CHRISTIANS
AND WAR

A. JAMES REIMER

CHRISTIANS AND WAR

A BRIEF HISTORY

Fortress Press
Minneapolis

CHRISTIANS AND WAR
A Brief History

Library of Congress Control Number: 2023933173 (print)

Cover image: Powerful detonator blast on the construction site
© Ghulam Hussain | iStock Photo
Cover design: Brice Hemmer

Print ISBN: 978-1-5064-8856-1
eBook ISBN: 978-1-5064-8857-8

Contents

Preface

Martin Luther's dilemma: "Can the Christian be a soldier?" or, more to the point, "Can a person who claims to follow Jesus Christ support and participate in violence even to defend oneself, one's family, and one's country?" has been a question that has plagued me ever since childhood. I remember carrying on a high school correspondence with a girlfriend half a country away on whether a Christian can go to war. I was unequivocally on the side of Christian pacifism but was unable to persuade her. My theological career has been to a large extent an attempt to answer this question.

This book is the fruit of many years of teaching both undergraduate and graduate students at Conrad Grebel University College (University of Waterloo in Ontario) and at the Toronto School of Theology. I acknowledge here the contribution of these students to making this a better work. I especially thank the students who participated in my course "War and Peace in Christian Thought" in 2006 and 2007 at the Toronto School of Theology. In those classes I used a rough draft of the manuscript for this book as my primary text, and the students gave me many helpful suggestions.

The purpose of the book is to present in summary, popular fashion a synthesis of materials chronicling the development of the church's arguments, teachings, and practices concerning Christian participation in violence, war, and peacemaking from the biblical period to the present, in a way that is accessible to nonspecialists. In the process I have been heavily reliant on some of the classic texts in the field, such as Roland H. Bainton, *Christian Attitudes toward War and Peace: A Historical Survey and Critical Re-evaluation* (1960); Lisa Sowle Cahill, *Love Your Enemies* (1994); and John H. Yoder, *Nevertheless: Varieties of Religious Pacifism* (1971) and *The Christian Witness to the State* (1964). Yoder's many writings on the subject have been a most important source in shaping the basic arguments and structure of the book, and my social ethics in general. Although I am not an uncritical "Yoderian," his influence is everywhere present, covertly if not explicitly.

I express my appreciation in particular to Fortress Press and editor Michael West for keeping faith with me through many delays and extensions, mostly due to ongoing health issues. I also acknowledge the assistance of a grant from the Social Sciences Humanities Research Council of Canada. A special thank you to my wife, Margaret Loewen Reimer, for her collaboration and skillful editing.

The intent was to keep this book as unencumbered as possible by lengthy footnotes, references, and quotations. Consequently, the usual scholarly apparatus has been kept to a minimum. Obvious dependencies have been noted in brief notes after the bibliography. I thank all those who have contributed to my understanding of the subject matter, especially my own Anabaptist-Mennonite heritage, which has highlighted the teachings of Jesus to "love the enemy," no matter what the cost.

As will become evident to a careful reader, my own pacifism is a chastened one, one that is only too aware of the ambiguities inherent in the nonresistant, pacifist position, especially when it comes to defending the third party through peacekeeping, peacemaking, and policing, activities to which I turn in the last chapter of the book. Nevertheless, I consider myself a *theological* pacifist—not a rigid, ideological one but one grounded in the Trinitarian-Christocentric love of God for the other and committed to the divine agenda of reconciling the whole fragmented world.

Introduction

On May 30, 1962, British composer Benjamin Britten conducted the premiere of his own work, the *War Requiem*, commissioned as part of the consecration of the rebuilt Coventry Cathedral in England. The fourteenth-century cathedral had suffered a direct hit by German bombers on November 15, 1940. The commission's intent was to recognize the need to end all war and work toward reconciliation among the nations of the world.[1]

Britten, a fervent pacifist, welcomed the opportunity to write a musical critique of war and decided to juxtapose nine poems by British poet William Owen with sections of the funeral liturgy (*Requiem*) of the Roman Catholic Church. Owen was a decorated army officer, awarded the Military Cross for bravery, who lost his life at the age of twenty-five, one week before the end of World War I. In his words, "The poetry is in the pity. . . . All a poet can do today is warn." Britten counterposed the personal anguish and anger of a soldier with the universal and timeless text of the Requiem Mass.

The high point of the *Requiem* comes with Owen's own version of the Abraham-Isaac story (based on Genesis 22:1-14), sung by tenor and baritone solo, in which God tests Abraham by commanding him to sacrifice his son:

> So Abram rose, and clave the wood, and went,
> And took the fire with him, and a knife.
> And as they sojourned both of them together,
> Isaac the first born spoke and said, My Father,
> Behold the preparations, fire and iron,
> But where the lamb for this burnt-offering?
> Then Abram bound the youth with belts and
>   straps,
> And builded parapets and trenched there,
> And stretched forth the knife to slay his son.
> When lo! An angel called him out of heaven,
> Saying, Lay not thy hand upon the lad,
> Neither do anything to him. Behold,
> A ram, caught in a thicket by its horns;
> Offer the Ram of Pride instead of him.
> But the old man would not so, but slew his son,—
> And half of the seed of Europe, one by one.

In an ironic reversal of the biblical narrative, which reads: "And Abraham went and took the ram, and offered it up as a burnt offering instead of his son" (Genesis 22:13), Owen's poem ends with Europe slaying thousands upon thousands of its precious sons. This, sadly, is the story of the twentieth century, which became one of unprecedented killing on the battlefields, the first century of all-out or "total" warfare, in which all the major powers were allied against one another, Christians fighting Christians, and Jews fighting Jews, all against all.

It has been estimated that approximately 231 million people died in conflicts and wars in the twentieth century. The outbreak of hostilities in August 1914 has sometimes been called the end of a century of "relative peace" that began with the signing of the Peace of Vienna in 1815. This picture of the nineteenth century as a time of peace does not do justice to the violence that was perpetrated during this period of history: the revolutions in Europe in 1848; the colonization of vast areas of India, China, Japan, and Africa by imperial powers, especially England, France, and Spain; the Civil War in the United States; the deportation and enslavement of Africans, especially by Americans; the domination of Aboriginal peoples and creation of "Indian reservations," and so on.

Nevertheless, it is true that the nineteenth century was a time of unprecedented faith in peace, human progress, missionary fervor, and optimism about the improvability of the world through science, reason, and international peace treaties. This optimism was still evident in the first year of World War I, when soldiers by the tens of thousands volunteered to fight for home and country, all sides under the banner of God's providential will. Many suffered disillusionment by the end of the year.

The German theologian Paul Tillich, who later emigrated to the United States under the threat of Nazism, experienced just such disillusionment. He too volunteered enthusiastically at the beginning of the "Great War to end all wars," to fight for his fatherland. But by the end of the first year, as a chaplain on the Western front, he suffered a nervous breakdown and lost his faith in traditional theism. Although he had been a firm believer in war as a struggle between nations and their right to exist, he soon came under the influence of Marxist thought, interpreting the war as an international class struggle. By war's end he was an advocate of "Religious Socialism," arguing that Christianity and socialism have much more in common than Christianity and capitalism.

It is the role that religion, and particularly Christianity, has played in war and peace-making throughout history that is the topic of this volume. Particular attention will be given to the theological teachings concerning war, violence, and peace that have motivated clergy, politicians, soldiers, military commanders, and ordinary people in their attitudes to war.

We will follow the career of the Christian church's attitudes toward war and peace from ancient Hebrew, Greek, and Roman times, the epoch in which the Jewish and Christian Bibles were written, through the classical period of Christian history (sometimes referred as the age of the "fathers"), the great Constantinian shift in the fourth century, the Middle Ages, the Reformation, and the early modern period with its religiously-inspired wars, to the era of modern "Enlightenment" and various contemporary perspectives. The goal here is not to present an exhaustive treatment of the subject, which one can find in numerous books, but rather to make accessible to the lay reader a sense of the central issues and arguments over the past two thousand years.

I cannot claim to be impartial, since I come from a longstanding pacifist tradition—the Anabaptist-Mennonite one—but I will attempt to be fair to all sides within the Christian tradition.

I'll let the reader judge whether I have managed it. In fact, it will become clear in the following pages, especially in the last chapters, that I am not an "absolute" pacifist (I do not reject all use of force), for I believe that some forms of peacekeeping and policing (to be distinguished from war) are necessary in the local, regional, national, and international arenas.

As mentioned above, this booklet is the product of some twenty years of teaching a course called "War and Peace in Christian Thought." I have come to recognize the importance of challenging students to take a personal interest in the topic and to write position papers in which they are required to take sides and to argue a position. This is difficult on any subject, but in the area of war and peace it is particularly onerous for those who have suffered the consequences of war personally or in their families. If I accomplish anything, I hope it is to challenge readers to think consciously about the subject and, theoretically at least, come to hold a position that is philosophically and religiously coherent, defensible and consistent with other areas of their lives, faithful to the Judeo-Christian tradition, and committed to a global humanism that promotes the peace and justice necessary to sustain the human and ecological environment of our world.

1

Definitions and Assumptions

This book offers an overarching view of the church's positions on war and peace through the centuries. To focus the discussion, we will rely on classifications and typologies, knowing that they sometimes undervalue the importance of particular situations and individual differences. But in a brief study such as this, typologies are indispensable. We will be structuring our treatment of the subject around five types of approaches to war: Pacifism, Crusade or Holy War, Just or Justifiable War, state self-interest (often referred to as *raison d'état*, by reason of state), and terrorism. The book ends with a theological consideration of "policing" as an alternative to war.

Before looking at approaches to war, however, some definitions are in order. My definitions of terms and concepts are not cut in stone but are working definitions that pertain to one type of violence (war) and only tangentially touch on other forms of violence, such as genocide, domestic and institutional abuse, capital punishment, abortion, homicide, suicide, and ecological violence.

Definitions

War, or armed conflict between nations or clashing factions within a country, is the most virulent and destructive form of violence. It is frequently justified as a necessary evil to defend freedom and justice, as a means of last resort to end even greater violence and restore peace, with lip service paid to rules of engagement and declarations of war. Yet wars are dependent on training camps, with instruction manuals, where young people are indoctrinated to think of other human beings as enemies and are trained to kill them.

Violence entails the "violation" of other human beings and of creation—inanimate or animate. It is the use of force (as in coercion, below) in a way that causes harm, injury, violation, or death. Force may be used deliberately to violate or to persuade people to do or not do something, or it may cause harm incidentally. Violation may be of a physical, psychological, spiritual, structural-systemic, or ecological variety.

Coercion is the use of force (or threat of force) to compel someone to do something or to restrain someone from doing something against his or her will. If it causes harm, it would be synonymous with violence; but coercion may be benign, devoid of harm, and even beneficial, as in disciplining children or restraining someone from committing suicide.

Power is frequently confused with violence or coercion, but it ought to be clearly distinguished from these. Power is the capacity to act, exert influence, and exercise authority, and it can function benevolently or malevolently. The exercise of power is necessary for the preservation of human existence and institutional life. It ranges from personal and humane authority in which individuals are dealt with as persons with dignity (as ideally in child discipline or community policing) to an impersonal and inhumane authority in which the dignity and value of the individual is no longer a factor (as in modern warfare and policing gone awry).

Policing, as I use it in this book, is to be distinguished from war and the military both in theory and in practice. It is used here as a kind of metaphor for efforts to preserve order and restrain violence against "innocent" populations within family, local, regional, national, and international arenas. Its primary goal is peacekeeping and peacemaking, and it is not premised on a training-culture of "killing" the other in any way comparable to military training. Although policing on rare occasions necessitates the use of lethal force, and sometimes deteriorates into abuse, its primary goal is to reduce violence and promote peace.

Pacifism is commonly taken to mean opposition to and refusal to participate in warfare or armed hostility of any kind. It may be personal or corporate (the ideology of a group or denomination). There are in fact many different types of pacifism, as we will discover below. Some pacifists are selective and limit their pacifism to certain groups, places, times, and conditions. Pacifism is often incorrectly identified with "passivism." This is unfortunate because most pacifists are committed to assertively resolving conflict by nonviolent peacemaking, negotiation, or mediation, and view reconciliation as a way of life.

Nonresistance is a radical form of pacifism that does not take a stand against or resist an aggressor. It is critical of any use of force to defend oneself or another, preferring to suffer and be persecuted ("turning the other cheek," as Jesus says) rather than to engage in any form of coercive activity. It is frequently held as a general attitude to all of life (a form of Christian discipleship) rather than merely the refusal to engage in warfare. The movie *Witness* portrays the Amish Mennonites as people who refuse to defend themselves when attacked. Whether nonresistance as a consistent approach to life is possible remains a debatable question.

Nonviolent resistance permits the use of benign, nonviolent force against an aggressor, or in defense of a third party, provided it does not cause harm, violation, or death to anyone. It may include protests, lobbying, boycotts, obstruction, Gandhian-type sit-downs, and sometimes damage to property. Any harm that occurs to people is not intentional.

To have clarity on these concepts is essential if one wants to do justice to the various historical and theological approaches to war and peace. Another important factor to keep in mind is that the Christian church's teachings and practices concerning war cannot be isolated from a much broader issue: that of the church's attitude to the wider world. This can be stated in terms of Christ and culture, church and state, or Christianity and society. How the church has understood its role in the broader society has determined its approaches to the issues of war, violence, and peace.

Church and Society

H. Richard Niebuhr, in his classic book *Christ and Culture*, identifies five types or ways of understanding the relationship of Christ to culture that he, sometimes mistakenly, identifies with specific denominations: Christ *against* culture, in which the church considers itself within society but not of it (as in "sects" like the Anabaptists); Christ *above* culture, in which the church tries to raise general culture to a higher Christ-like level (as in medieval Roman Catholicism, which viewed grace as transcending nature); Christ *and* culture in paradoxical juxtaposition, where both church and society require allegiance but exist on different planes (as in traditional Lutheranism); Christ *of* culture, where the church uncritically identifies with culture (as in nineteenth-century liberal Protestantism, particularly German "Culture-Protestantism"); and Christ *transforming* culture, where the church is engaged in society in an effort to bring about greater justice (as in the Reformed-Calvinist tradition).

Niebuhr's typology, which has had a profound influence on American denominational understanding of the church's relation to the surrounding world, is an instance where "ideal types" are both helpful and distorting of particular traditions. It has been helpful in provoking Christians to examine seriously where they stand on a variety of issues related to the "Christ and culture" duality, including war and violence. It has also in some instances led to distorted views of others. For example, it classifies Anabaptist-Mennonites as an instance of "Christ against culture," when in fact historically Anabaptist-Mennonites see themselves as providing a radical alternative culture of peace to the dominant violent culture. There are strong transformative elements in this counter-culture tradition.

Niebuhr himself sides with the Reformed "Christ the transformer of culture" type and in so doing is prone to caricaturing the other types, implicitly assuming that they are all static approaches when in fact each of them has dynamic elements. Furthermore, his list of types is incomplete. In a recent conversation, a theologian of Reformed background suggested to me a sixth type to add to Niebuhr's list: "Christ the subverter of culture." He said that Reformed theologians always talk about "Christ the transformer of culture," but there are times when culture is so corrupted that to be faithful to Christ means to subvert that culture so that it can be more radically transformed, or even replaced.

I have in my own work argued for a seventh type: one in which the boundaries between

Christ and culture, church and world, Christian and state are more fluid, possibly requiring any one of the above six types on different occasions. The Christian's primary home is the believing community (the church), and the secondary home is the world beyond that community. Fidelity to Christ requires a moving into the world and withdrawing from the world in dynamic ways that may require on different occasions blessing culture, raising culture to a higher level, standing in a paradoxical relation to culture, positioning oneself over against culture, and even subverting or transforming culture. In short, the church-world categories ought not to be considered static types but dynamic positions.

Approaches to War

What does the church's attitude to society have to do with war and peace? How one views the church's role in culture and in the world will have ramifications for how one understands the church's stance toward war and policing. How one approaches the issue of violence socially and ethically has to do with how one views one's relation to, and responsibility for, the world. Each of the above church-society models might evoke different responses to whether one is willing to participate in military engagement or not. In this study, we will be looking primarily at the three approaches to war that have most relevance for the Christian Church: holy war or crusade, just war or justifiable war, and pacifism.

Holy war or *crusade* is a war fought either in obedience to divine command or with special divine assistance, as in having "God on our side." Some view the crusade as an example of God's command and holy war as claiming "God on our side." In this volume, I will as a rule not make this distinction and will use the terms interchangeably. Tracing the career of the holy war through history, one could say it was dominant in certain periods of Jewish history (as narrated in the Hebrew scriptures) and in the apocalyptic literature of the New Testament (as in the imagery of the book of Revelation). It was evoked in the high to late Middle Ages (eleventh to thirteenth century), in some Reformation groups (some of the rhetoric of the Reformed tradition and some factions within the Radical Reformers), and in the religious wars of the post-Reformation (seventeenth century), sometimes referred to as the "Age of Intolerance" and "dogmatism."

In the twentieth century, much of the war rhetoric of World War I, on both sides, had a "crusade" quality, as did some liberation movements. In all of the above cases, clear lines are drawn between light and darkness, good and evil, those who have God on their side and those who do not, the righteous and the unrighteous, the oppressed and the oppressor. Effectiveness is not the primary consideration in these movements, only obedience to divine command and will, with frequent appropriation of martyrdom language. Terrorist movements in our century frequently employ the language of holy war or crusade (see chapter 12).

Just war or *justifiable war*, as it was first considered in the period of Augustine of Hippo (early fifth century), was a war fought out of necessity, subject to certain conditions. To call a war *justifiable* was to recognize war as a sin for which one had to repent but which nevertheless was unavoidable due to the fallenness of the world and of human activity. It was, one might say, a "lesser evil," no perfect choice being available. In this kind of thinking, war is wrong; and the burden of proof lies with the one deciding to wage war. Just war language, on the other hand, has the ring of a more positive attitude to war, as a duty of Christians and the church under certain conditions.

It has been suggested by Mennonite theologian and ethicist John Howard Yoder that war prior to the sixteenth-century Reformation fell under the category of justifiable war, while after the Reformation war took on the more positive meaning which found its way into mainline church confessions. This has been disputed, but it is helpful to recognize the distinction between justifiable and just war. We will for the most part treat them interchangeably.

Just war thinking was present already within the Greek city-states. In the Christian tradition, it has roots in the Judeo-Christian scriptures. In western Christianity, it arises more formally in the fourth and fifth centuries with Ambrose and Augustine, as part of the so-called Constantinian shift, when Christianity became the dominant religion. In the Middle Ages, it was the dominant Catholic position and was revived among the city-states in Renaissance Italy.

The just war has strong defenders in the mainline groups of the Reformation, regaining strength in the twentieth century, particularly during and after World War II. It continues to have strong proponents among theological ethicists such as Paul Ramsey and Oliver O'Donovan. The just war tradition has in its historical career developed a typical set of conditions both for declaring war (*jus ad bellum*) and for fighting war (*jus in bello*). These conditions or criteria leading up to war and determining what is acceptable within war will be considered in greater detail below (see chapter 5).

Pacifism is a third type of approach to the question of war. Important to note is the fact that there are many forms of pacifism, all assuming that war and violence are wrong but differing in the underlying motivation and justification for espousing a pacifist stance. Mennonite scholar John Howard Yoder, one of the most influential defenders of pacifism in the twentieth century, tenaciously challenged the reduction of pacifism to "passivism" or to a single approach.

In his booklet *Nevertheless: The Varieties of Religious Pacifism*, Yoder identifies more than twenty-five different types of pacifism, including the Roman Catholic "Pacifism of Christian Cosmopolitanism" (espoused by Pope John XXIII in his *Pacem in Terris*), which assumes a common, global humanity and the priority of pastoral concern; and the just war "Pacifism of the Honest Study of Cases," where each case must be considered separately to see whether it is justifiable. Other types include "The Pacifism of Absolute Principle" (the imperative not to kill, grounded in the authority of scripture); "The Pacifism of Nonviolent Social Change" (the use of pacifist pressure to bring about justice, represented by Mohandas K. Gandhi and Martin Luther King Jr.); and "The Pacifism of the Virtuous Minority" (represented by Menno Simons, who espoused a nonresistant, nonconforming community). Yoder's own "Pacifism of the Messianic Community" is grounded in the Incarnation: It presupposes a corporate confession of Jesus Christ as Lord in which the person and work of Christ translate into a dynamic enemy-loving way of life in the context of a community of discipleship.

In the 1992 expanded edition of *Nevertheless*, Yoder identifies the Jewish nonviolence tradition after Jeremiah as foreshadowing later Christian pacifism, calling it "The Pacifism of Rabbinic Monotheism." He argues provocatively, although a bit too one-sidedly, that "For two and a half millennia, from Josiah to Ben Gurion, Jewry represents the longest and strongest experience of religious-cultural-moral continuity in known history, defended without the sword."

While Yoder's many forms of pacifism provide helpful distinctions, the sheer number of types tends to relativize the very notion of pacifism as a category. For our purposes, one might divide Yoder's types into two major ones: (1) *political or liberal pacifism*, which seeks pragmatically to use pacifism as a means of transforming society, based on an optimistic view of human nature and of history; and (2) *biblical pacifism*, which is grounded in the person and teachings of Christ, committed to transforming society toward peace, justice, and reconciliation through nonviolent means without illusion about human perfectibility and historical progress.

The idealization of peace has been strong in many historical periods and traditions. In Judaism, *shalom* is thought of as a state of peace and total well-being. The Greek word for peace (*eirene*) refers to a state of order and harmony. In the Roman period, *Pax Romana* was understood as the absence of war and military conflict. The early Christian church was in principle opposed to the shedding of blood and participation in the military. During the sixteenth-century Reformation, pacifist groups emerged within certain wings of the Radical Reformation. In the modern period, eighteenth-century Enlightenment saw the rise of pacifism in the great humanist tradition. The period between World War I and World War II saw renewed calls for the church to reject all war, and in the second half of the twentieth century, there were strong pacifist movements in most major Christian denominations.

State self-interest (*raison d'état*), a fourth type of approach to war, does not emerge from religious roots like the other three—it is not based on moral or Christian ethical reasoning but is a pragmatic-realist approach to violence and war. It assumes that the state has its own superior reason by which it can use violence based on self-interest and self-preservation, regardless of moral reasoning. Although throughout history states have used holy war and just war rhetoric ideologically to underpin their militarism, a candid analysis would show that most wars have been fought "by reason of state"—for purely national, economic, political, or other "non-moral" reasons. As we shall see below, the first three types—holy war/crusade, just/justifiable war, pacifism—may be said to have biblical warrants. But this fourth type cannot be so defended. Although religion has often been used ideologically to support a war that is waged primarily on grounds of state self-interest, this type will not figure strongly in the following pages.

Whether "terror" and the "war on terror" can be considered an additional type of approach to war is an issue we will consider in chapter 12. Chapter 13 will look at policing as an alternative to war.

2

Hebrew Scriptures:
God of War and God of Peace

Biblical texts can be found to illustrate all three of the main positions concerning Christian attitudes to violence and war: holy war, just war, and pacifism. Consequently, in order to avoid moral relativism, one needs to develop a coherent position on theological grounds rather than arguing from individual texts alone.

In the following pages we will look at the tensions that exist between various texts in the Hebrew and Christian scriptures and identify the ways in which various theological and historical traditions have sought to resolve these tensions through a coherent hermeneutics (interpretation). In this chapter, we examine the variety of texts in the Hebrew Scriptures (or Old Testament, as it is known to Christians). All biblical references in this book are from the New Revised Standard Version.

God as Holy Warrior

First, we look at the holy war position, remembering the distinction between a God-commanded war and a God-supported war. Throughout the Hebrew scriptures one finds texts in which God is described as a "holy warrior," one who commands that his people commit violent acts toward the enemy, himself commits such violent acts, or comes to the aid of his people in times of war. (I am using the male pronoun for God here because this is the dominant image of God in the Hebrew scriptures.)

The most dramatic of the texts describing God as holy or tribal warrior can be found in Exodus 15:

> I will sing to the Lord, for he has triumphed
>   gloriously;
> horse and rider he has thrown into the sea.
> The Lord is my strength and my might,
> and he has become my salvation;
> this is my God, and I will praise him,
> my father's God, and I will exalt him.
> The Lord is a warrior;
> the Lord is his name.

This is the song of Moses and Miriam, sung after crossing the Red Sea (or Reed Sea), where Pharaoh's army has been drowned by the returning waters—"not one of them remained" (14:28). This violent event follows the story of God killing the Egyptian first-born sons, the last of the ten plagues that are to show the power of God, a power which is not reliant on the military strength of his people.

The mighty power of God is a theme that is present throughout the "violent" passages in the Old Testament: the miraculous triumph of God's chosen people over the enemy, even though vastly outnumbered and with inferior weapons. In Psalm 33:16-19 we read: "A king is not saved by his great army; a warrior is not delivered by his great strength. The war horse is a vain hope for victory, and by its great might it cannot save. Truly the eye of the Lord is on those who fear him, on those who hope in his steadfast love, to deliver their soul from death, and to keep them alive in famine."

Second Kings 9 and 10 tell the story of the divinely commanded massacre of seventy sons of Ahab. The Psalmist frequently calls upon God to avenge Israel and kill the enemy, even while acknowledging that God hates violence. "The Lord tests the righteous and the wicked, and his soul hates the lover of violence. On the wicked he will rain coals of fire and sulphur; a scorching wind shall be the portion of their cup" (11:5-6). We have direct commands of God to slaughter the enemy: "Thus says the Lord of hosts, 'I will punish the Amalekites for what they did in opposing the Israelites when they came out of Egypt. Now go and attack Amalek, and utterly destroy all that they have; do not spare them, but kill both man and woman, infant and suckling, ox and sheep, camel and donkey'" (1 Samuel 15:2-3). And God even wreaks violence on his own chosen ones: "The Lord has done what he purposed, he has carried out his threat. . . . The young and the old are lying on the ground in the streets; my young women and my young men have fallen by the sword; in the day of your anger you have killed them, slaughtering without mercy" (Lamentations 2:17, 21). Yet the next chapter reiterates confidence in God's steadfast love.

So we see a constant tension, even within texts that would seem to support a holy war, between a God who wills violence and one who hates violence. On the one hand, God is praised as the one who "trains my hand for war, so that my arms can bend a bow of bronze" (Psalm 18:34), and on the other as the God who "makes wars cease to the end of the earth . . . breaks the bow, and shatters the spear [and] burns the shields with fire" (46:9).

A Just War Prototype

Second, we find some texts that might be said to foreshadow just war reasoning, even though these texts still fall within a holy war tradition. The just war approach states that the declaration of war (*ad bellum*) and the actual fighting of war (*in bello*) are to be governed by certain rules and conditions, begun to be articulated during the Constantinian era, as we shall see in chapter 5. However, we do find a prototype of just war thinking earlier, in the classical period of Greek humanism as well as in the Old Testament.

In 2 Chronicles 28, the people of Israel are rebuked for waging war too enthusiastically. God has sanctioned their attack on Judah (a just end) but Israel has "killed them in a rage that has reached up to heaven" (unjust means). Israel is ordered to give up its plunder and send the prisoners home, providing food and clothing for the journey.

In Deuteronomy 20–26 we find war and violence sanctioned conditionally.[1] The Deuteronomical rules include conditions that apply to the time leading up to war and to conduct within war. There are hints of what later just war theorists call "just authority:" Priests are to encourage the people not to be afraid but to trust in God ("just intent and motivation");

military officers are to tell potential soldiers to first take care of unfinished business at home (look after a new house, satisfy the needs of a new wife, look after the vineyard); commanders are appointed to lead the people going into war. Before engaging in combat, peace terms are to be offered to the enemy—if they accept, the lives of the enemy are to be spared and used as forced labor.

If the enemy refuses peace terms, military engagement is justified under the following rules of conduct: all males are to be killed and spoils taken, although a distinction is made between distant nations and nations nearby who become the inheritance of Israel—in the latter case nothing that breathes is to be left (this includes the Hittites, Amorites, Canaanites and other peoples of the Promised Land), so that non-Jewish people will not corrupt Israel's faith and practices. There are even rules about nature—when besieging a city, soldiers are not to destroy fruit trees but may cut down other trees for military use.

Blood was considered sacred by the Hebrews, and detailed prescriptions are given on how to treat the body of an innocent man, including the sacrifice of a heifer to atone for the sin of shedding innocent blood: "'Absolve, O Lord, your people Israel, whom you redeemed; do not let the guilt of innocent blood remain in the midst of your people Israel.' Then they will be absolved of blood guilt. So you shall purge the guilt of innocent blood from your midst, because you must do what is right in the sight of the Lord" (Deut. 21:8-9).

Should an Israelite desire a beautiful woman from the enemy, he must give her time to mourn her parents before taking her for a wife, not enslaving her but giving her freedom to go where she pleases. Deuteronomy 21–26 is a series of detailed rules on how to deal with other violence-related issues: rebellious sons, capital punishment (don't let a body hang on a tree for more than a day), how to treat strangers and even wildlife (birds). Also listed are rules concerning sexual relations, marriage and divorce, escaped slaves, prostitution, tithing and usury/interest (it may be charged to a foreigner but not to a fellow Israelite).

A primary concern in all of the above is cultic purity: "When you are encamped against your enemies you shall guard against any impropriety" (23:9). There is even a statement on what later came to be called "proportionality": "If the one in the wrong deserves to be flogged, the judge shall make that person lie down and be beaten in his presence with the number of lashes proportionate to the offense" (25:2).

Pacifist Motifs

Third, we find in the Hebrew Scriptures texts that support "pacifistic" readings. In addition to those passages that we have looked at in connection with the holy war and just war traditions, we find others that explicitly denounce all war, and perceive God and his people as suffering violence rather than perpetrating violence. The later prophetic texts begin to understand God less as a tribal or holy warrior, and more as one who, together with his chosen people, fits the role of the "suffering servant." This is perhaps most dramatically illustrated in Isaiah 53, a passage made famous in Handel's *Messiah*, especially in the poignant aria, "He was despised and rejected of men," and the moving choruses "Behold the Lamb of God" and "Surely He hath borne our griefs." This Isaiah text has been variously interpreted as pointing to Israel as representing the suffering servant, or as the prophetic foreshadowing of Christ and his suffering on the cross.

Isaiah 53 conveys a new understanding of God as the one who is present within suffering humanity. The servant of God is depicted as one who is without beauty, despised and rejected by humanity, a "man of sorrows" who has borne the grief of others. This suffering servant has even been "smitten by God," but by his punishing stripes we are healed. He went like a lamb to the slaughter without opening his mouth, and "although he had done no violence," he was "numbered among the transgressors" and was "stricken for the transgression of [God's] people."

This nonviolent servant depicts the divine character of God himself and, together with similar passages, provides a counterpoint to the violent, vengeful God we find in other Hebrew texts. The same prophet, Isaiah, prophesies of a time when God "will judge between the nations, and shall arbitrate for many peoples; they shall beat their swords into plowshares, and their spears into pruning hooks; nation shall not lift up sword against nation, neither shall they learn war any more" (Isaiah 2:4).

Micah 4:3-4 has a similar vision of the future: God "shall judge between many peoples, and shall arbitrate for between strong nations afar away; they shall beat their swords into plowshares, and their spears into pruning hooks; nation shall not lift up sword against nation, neither shall they learn war any more; but they shall all sit every one under their own vines and under their own fig trees, and no one shall make them afraid; for the mouth of the Lord of hosts has spoken." These passages inspired the Soviet Union, at the height of the

Cold War, to donate to the United Nations a sculpture of a heroic figure beating a sword into a plowshare.

Another biblical voice, however, uses the same images in an opposing messianic vision. The prophet Joel calls for plowshares to become swords in his call to war: "Proclaim this among the nations; Prepare war, stir up the warriors. Let all the soldiers draw near, let them come up. Beat your plowshares into swords, and your pruning hooks into spears; let the weakling say, 'I am a warrior'" (3:9-10).

Reconciling Diverse Texts

We have looked at three sets of texts which can be, and have been, used to justify three different approaches to war and peace among God's people. How can these seemingly contradictory texts be incorporated into one coherent whole? Various attempts have been made to reconcile what at first appear to be irreconcilable views of God and God's intention for his people and the world. I will consider five here and end with my own proposal.

Supersessionism. One attempt at resolving the tensions between apparently conflicting texts is Christian supersessionism. This view holds that Jesus Christ, the apostles, and the Christian church supersede, even replace, the Old Testament heroes of faith, the prophets, and Israel as God's people. The most extreme form of supersessionism is identified with the second-century bishop, Marcion, who was one of the first to collect New Testament writings. His intent was to exclude the Old Testament or Hebrew Bible from the Christian scriptures and to expunge all references to the Old Testament in Christian writings. He believed that the God of the Old Testament (a God of wrath) was a different God than that of the New Testament (the God of Jesus Christ and of love).

The early church had the wisdom, after considerable debate, to reject the Marcionite position and to include in the Christian canon both the Hebrew Bible and New Testament. Marcionism continues to subtly influence certain theological streams within contemporary theology and is a temptation for some pacifists, including some in my own Anabaptist-Mennonite heritage. Supersessionism was a prevalent view prior to the twentieth century, after which it came under severe criticism for its potential anti-Semitic or anti-Judaic assumptions.

Fourfold Hermeneutics. A second attempt to reconcile diverse texts is the ancient fourfold method of interpreting the Bible: (1) the *literal* (not literalistic in the modern sense) way of reading, which was the common sense or straightforward approach; (2) the *allegorical*, a spiritual or mystical reading; (3) the *tropological*, a moral and ethical reading; and (4) the *anagogical*, a future-oriented reading. Origen, the great third-century Alexandrian theologian, who was a pacifist, was fond of finding hidden spiritual and mystical meanings behind texts, and he used this approach to interpret difficult militaristic texts in the Old Testament. Thus a pacifist could take the Old Testament texts that appear on the literal level to justify a holy war and reinterpret them in a spiritual sense, as in "spiritual warfare." Difficulties or contradictions can be reconciled by recognizing different levels of interpretation.

Dispensationalism. A third way to reconcile conflicting texts is known as Dispensationalism. This view sees Judeo-Christian history as divided into seven dispensations or divine periods of time, with certain texts meant for certain periods. This was an ingenious way of interpreting the Bible, prevalent among some Christian groups in the late nineteenth and early twentieth centuries (groups sometimes referred to as "Fundamentalists" because of their literalistic way of reading the Bible). Each dispensation ended with a crisis and was then replaced with a new dispensation.

Because different texts are meant for different eras, they can be interpreted literally as God's will without contradicting each other. For example, militaristic texts could be understood as referring to a different era than pacifistic ones. Interestingly, a contemporary version of theological interpretation, the "paradigm" approach to Christian history, also takes different historical epochs seriously for hermeneutics. This approach is associated with theologians Hans Küng and David Tracy. Although quite different from dispensationalist theory, this paradigm approach also sees epochs of interpretation transitioning from one to another through periods of crisis, based on dramatically new assumptions for reading texts and historical events.

Progressive Revelation. Fourth, the concept of progressive revelation could be a way of reconciling seemingly contradictory texts. This is a milder version of the supersessionist view, putting forward the idea that God reveals the divine character and will to people gradually, over time. Thus the older revelation of God as vengeful, wrathful, and warrior-like moves gradually to a later understanding of God as nonviolent, nonvengeful and loving, a God who is opposed to war. Christians might interpret the coming of Christ, with his nonviolent, nonresistant life and teachings, culminating in his death on the cross, as the apex of this progressive revelation. Sixteenth-century Reformer John Calvin's concept of "accommodation" could be seen as a form of this view—that God accommodates divine revelation to the readiness of human beings to understand and receive that revelation. What distinguishes the progressive revelation approach from Calvin's accommodation view is that the former might presuppose the modern notion of progress—the idea that human beings become gradually more knowledgeable and intellectually more able to understand the will of God. Calvin did not assume this kind of human progress. A difficulty with the progressive revelation view is that some later biblical texts are more militaristic than earlier ones.

Historical-Critical Method. Fifth, the historical-critical method of interpreting the Bible has been dominant in the modern period of western philosophical and theological thought. To oversimplify, it might be divided into an earlier historical-critical approach and a later canonical-critical one. The historical-critical approach (including historical criticism, form criticism, and redaction criticism) was rooted in Enlightenment assumptions concerning religious texts and language. It was concerned with discovering what was originally meant, and with dissecting and analyzing the variety of books, and the diversity of smaller units within books.

It sometimes tended to second-guess biblical authors and traditions (we know better what was going on than the original writers did).

In this kind of reading, war texts as well as pacifistic texts could be relativized. The critic might conclude that when we are told "God said," we need not take this at face value; human beings assumed they heard God speaking. In the same way, historical critics might assume that human editors put their own agendas into the mouth of God. In this kind of reading, conflicting texts are not a serious problem but are seen as historical-human utterances in different contexts. The historical-critical method has made a great contribution to our understanding of the biblical world but is prone to focus on smaller segments of scripture rather than the overall scope.

The examination of the scriptures as a whole, emphasizing unifying theological and literary themes as a way of reading a diversity of texts, is the task of the canonical-critical approach and what is sometimes referred to as Biblical Theology. Many recent scholars examining the holy war tradition within the Old Testament are using a canonical method in which the theology of the Old and New Testaments are seen to witness to a "universal redemptive drama." The unity behind texts which seem to stand in tension with each other lies in the unity of the divine agent guiding this dramatic narrative. Like other peoples of the ancient Near East, Israel saw the world as situated dangerously between order and chaos, always in danger of slipping back into chaos and conflict. Where Israel differed from its neighbors is that it envisioned an eschatological (future) kingdom of peace, understood not simply as the absence of war but as *shalom*: a state of health, wholeness, mercy, and justice, where lamb and lion would lie down together, and where there would be no more war. The biblical perspective of *shalom* was meant not only for Israel but for the world in its entirety. War was itself a fight against chaos or a slipping back into chaos.

An Old Testament scholar from my own Mennonite tradition, Millard Lind, has sought to give an alternative reading of the violent texts of the Hebrew scriptures using the historical-critical method but also remaining faithful to his pacifist convictions. In his provocative book, *Yahweh Is a Warrior,* Lind argues, against common assumptions, that the earliest patriarchal period of Israel's history was essentially pacifist in character. Only with the poetry and narratives of the Exodus is there a more aggressive concern for justice amidst conflict, introducing the rhetoric of violence. What distinguished Israel's exodus material from that of neighboring nations, however, was that "the Hebrew clans were not called to do battle in the usual sense of the word, but to respond to and trust in Yahweh as sole warrior against the military might of Egypt. The Hebrew freedom movement experienced Yahweh as the sole bearer of a unique political power and authority addressed both to themselves and their enemy through a prophetic personality."

This Hebrew understanding, based on prophetic personality rather than military leadership, was "a new type of theo-political order, the kingship of Yahweh." Only gradually do the Israelites clamor after a monarchical structure of political rule comparable to that of their neighbors, but it remains in constant tension with the radical prophetic vision of rule by Yahweh. Jesus and his followers, in contrast to the Zealots, and before them the Maccabees, sought to return to the pacifistic message of the prophets. Lind's proposal sheds valuable light on the difference between Israel's early dependence on Yahweh's miraculous intervention in their historical and military adventures, and their reliance on centralized military establishments like their neighboring nations. Nevertheless, it begs the question of the warlike nature of God's own character in the Hebrew scriptures and how human agency is involved instrumentally in the exercise of violence on behalf of God. An alternative to the attempts to harmonize conflicting voices of scripture is simply to assume that the Hebrew Bible is pluralistic and accommodates a variety of points of view, reflecting the ongoing arguments over the centuries about the nature of Yaweh.

A Trinitarian Reading

This brings me to my own attempt to deal with the diversity of Old Testament texts. I propose a Trinitarian reading of the entire Bible. It is not meant to replace historical-critical hermeneutics, nor aspects of the other solutions considered above. It has much in common with the canonical approach, based on the assumption that behind the diverse texts is a living, divine agent. This is self-consciously a Christian interpretation of both the Hebraic and the New Testament texts.

A Trinitarian hermeneutic seeks to hold together all the three sets of texts we have been discussing (those on holy war, just war, and pacifism) as representing various manifestations of God: the mystery of God in God's hidden purposes for the world, God's will in Jesus the Christ, and God's life-giving power in the Spirit. Although the three "persons" of the Trinity—Father, Son, and Spirit—are three ways of being of the one God (diversity within unity), each of the three represents aspects of the divine nature: (1) God the Father represents the unbegotten and mysterious origin of all things, the one who has power over life and death, and can in his hidden way turn violence (which in itself is evil) into good, and thereby bring about the providential divine purpose; (2) God the Son or Word as incarnated in Jesus the Christ reveals the mystery of redemption through nonviolent love and the cross, the reconciliation of God and humanity, and embodies the standard for all Christian ethics; and (3) the Holy Spirit as the great reconciler and sanctifier who is the mysterious source of life, power, and reconciliation of all things separated by sin and the fall.

These are not three gods but One God moving and working in three different ways, ways that sometimes seem to our mortal minds to conflict with one another. But in a very real sense each of the three "persons" are involved in all three ways. We will have occasion to draw out more of the implications of a Trinitarian theology later in this volume.

3

New Testament:
Jesus and Loving the Enemy

The New Testament scriptures do not speak to the issue of war as directly as the Hebrew scriptures. The New Testament emerges out of a different kind of community than much of the Old Testament; these later writers do not presuppose a theocratic kingship with centralized decision-making powers but speak to a community of the Diaspora, a persecuted minority dispersed throughout the Roman Empire. Nevertheless, the New Testament too has a variety of texts that have been used to justify each of the three approaches to war and peace—holy war, just war, and pacifism. This chapter will identify these sets of texts and trace historical attempts to deal with them, without entering too deeply into exegetical and hermeneutical scholarship regarding various passages.

Holy War Texts

There are passages in the New Testament that sound as though they justify aggressive or militant use of the sword to bring in God's kingdom, the center of Jesus' preaching. In John 2 we read of business transactions and money-changing being conducted in the outer courts of the Temple during the Passover in Jerusalem. Jesus becomes angry and uses a whip to overturn the tables of the money-changers and drives them out of the Temple with the words: "Take these things out of here! Stop making my Father's house a marketplace" (John 2:15, 16). We find another perplexing text in Matthew 10:34-39:

> Do not think that I have come to bring peace to the earth; I have not come to bring peace, but a sword. For I have come to set a man against his father, and a daughter against her mother, and a daughter-in-law against her mother-in-law; and one's foes will be members of one's own household. Whoever loves father or mother more than me is not worthy of me; and whoever loves son or daughter more than me is not worthy of me; and whoever does not take the cross and follow me is not worthy of me. Those who find their life will lose it, and those who lose their life for my sake will find it.

It should be noted that the above passage follows upon a peaceful meditation by Jesus on the value of life: "Do not fear those who kill the body but cannot kill the soul; rather fear him who can destroy both soul and body in hell. Are not two sparrows sold for a penny? Yet not one of them will fall to the ground apart your Father. And even the hairs of your head are all counted" (Matthew 10:28-31).

Another text that falls into the same genre as the ones above is Luke 22:35-38:

> He said to them [his disciples], "When I sent you out without a purse, bag, or sandals, did you lack anything?" They said, "No, not a thing." He said to them, "But now, the one who has a purse must take it, and likewise a bag. And the one who has no sword must sell his cloak and buy one. For I tell you, this scripture must be fulfilled in me, 'And he was counted among the lawless'; and indeed what is written about me is being fulfilled." They said, "Lord, look, here are two swords." He replied, "It is enough."

Again, exegetes with varying positions have interpreted this text in ways that support their theological convictions about the church's stance on war and nonviolence. For our purposes we will let them stand as they are, difficult texts which cannot easily be argued away or softened.

The most militant "holy war" New Testament texts can be found in the Apocalypse of John, the book of Revelation. Here we have the most graphic picture of God's final judgment against those who have persecuted the elect: shocking images of the seven plagues or "seven bowls of the wrath of God" administered by seven angels (Revelation 16 and 17). We read of foul sores, the sea and rivers turned into blood killing everything in them, the sun scorching people with fire as they "gnawed their tongues in agony." We read of "demonic spirits, performing signs, who go abroad to the kings of the whole world, to assembly them for battle on the great day of God the Almighty." The text warns of the divine "coming like a thief" and calls for vigilance. We hear of a multitude assembled for the final battle at a place called Armageddon. (The name refers to the Mountain of Megiddo, the site of many ancient battles.)

Finally, with the seventh angel comes a great earthquake: "The great city was split into three parts, and the cities of the nations fell. God remembered great Babylon and gave her the wine-cup of the fury of his wrath. And every island fled away, and no mountains were to be found; and huge hailstones, each weighing about a hundred pounds, dropped from heaven on people, until they cursed God for the plague of the hail, so fearful was that plague" (16:17-21). The book of Revelation is full of such warlike language and violent symbolism of divine judgment, which has been used by literalistic, chiliastic (apocalyptic) leaders to rally the troops in the battle against evil. One can also interpret these texts metaphorically and allegorically, but the horrific violence of the images remains troublesome.

Just War Texts

A second group of New Testament passages has been used in defense of just war thinking. Even though the "rules" of the just war are not present, the conditional obedience to the government even in the use of the sword, presupposed by these texts, gives them a "just war" character. The most frequently cited passage in this regard is Romans 13:1-7:

> Let every person be subject to the governing authorities; for there is no authority except from God, and those authorities that exist have been instituted by God. Therefore whoever resists authority resists what God has appointed, and those who resist will incur judgment. For rulers are not a terror to good

conduct, but to bad. Do you wish to have no fear of the authority? Then do what is good, and you will receive its approval; for it is God's servant for your good. But if you do what is wrong, you should be afraid, for the authority does not bear the word in vain! It is the servant of God to execute wrath on the wrongdoer. Therefore one must be subject, not only because of wrath but also because of conscience. For the same reason you also pay taxes, for the authorities are God's servants, busy with this very thing. Pay to all what is due them—taxes to whom taxes are due, revenue to whom revenue is due, respect to whom respect is due, honor to whom honor is due.

A similar text is found in 1 Peter 2:13-17:

For the Lord's sake accept the authority of every human institution, whether of the emperor as supreme, or of governors, as sent by him to punish those who do wrong and praise those who do right. For it is God's will that by doing right you should silence the ignorance of the foolish. As servants of God, live as free people, yet do not use your freedom as a pretext for evil. Honor everyone. Love the family of believers. Fear God. Honor the emperor.

Another much-interpreted text that gives limited legitimacy to civil authority and government is Mark 12:17, where Jesus tells his followers to "Render to Caesar the things that are Caesar's, and to God the things that are God's." In the Lukan writings (the Gospel of Luke and the Book of Acts) the author shows a "friendliness" to civil rulers not present in many other New Testament writings.

Pacifist Texts

Passages that encourage obedience to ruling authorities who are called to maintain law and order, even with the sword, stand side by side in the New Testament with passages that extol peace, love, and nonresistance. Take for example the Romans 13 passage. It is juxtaposed with a passage just before it, Romans 12:14-21, which appears to be saying the opposite:

> Bless those who persecute you; bless and do not curse them. . . . Do not repay anyone evil for evil, but take thought for what is noble in the sight of all. If it is possible, so far as it depends upon you, live peaceably with all. Beloved, never avenge yourselves, but leave room for the wrath of God; for it is written, "Vengeance is mine, I will repay, says the Lord." No, "if your enemies are hungry, feed them; if they are thirsty, give them something

to drink; for by doing this you will heap burn-
ing coals on their heads." Do not be overcome
by evil, but overcome evil with good.

How can these two disparate passages—one
urging obedience to civil authority even in its
use of force, the other calling for nonresistant love—be reconciled? We shall later in this
chapter examine various theological attempts
to address such conflicting biblical injunctions.

A strong case can be made on the basis of
the New Testament for nonresistant pacifism.
We have already noted the "suffering servant"
motif in the Hebrew scriptures, and Romans
12:14-21, which urges love of enemy. Now we
turn to the most important text for pacifism,
the Sermon on the Mount of Matthew 5-7,
which includes the Beatitudes. The most significant for us are the six precepts of Jesus
in Matthew 5:21-48, sometimes referred to as
the "hard sayings of Jesus." Following Jesus'
words, "Do not think that I have come to abolish the law or the prophets; I have come not
to abolish but to fulfill" (5:17), Jesus states
the law on six different issues and gives six
alternative imperatives.

The first, fifth, and sixth are the most relevant for this discussion: (1) It has been said
in the law that "You shall not murder," but

Jesus says, "If you are angry with a brother or sister, you will be liable to judgment" (5:21-22). (2) The law demands "an eye for an eye and a tooth for a tooth" (*lex talionis*), but Jesus responds: "Do not resist an evildoer. But if any one strikes you on the right cheek, turn the other also" (5:38-39). (3) The law says, "You shall love your neighbor and hate your enemy," but Jesus retorts: "Love your enemies and pray for those who persecute you, so that you may be children of your Father in heaven" (5:43-45). In each case Jesus' demands are loftier and more demanding than those of the Old Testament law. These six precepts follow the Beatitudes, where the suffering of the righteous (recalling the Hebrew scriptures) is enjoined: "Blessed are the peacemakers, for they will be called children of God. Blessed are those who are persecuted for righteousness' sake, for theirs is the kingdom of heaven" (5:9-10).

These texts, when combined with the life and example of Jesus himself, lend powerful support to the Christian pacifist option. Jesus chose the way of the cross rather than earthly power (in Matthew 4 he is tempted by various earthly vocations of power), and in his crucifixion he takes on the form of a suffering servant. The Christian way is ultimately one of love and reconciliation, not hate and hostility.

Attempts at Harmonization

Various proposals throughout history have attempted to harmonize these diverse texts, which on the surface seem to be in outright contradiction. Let us take Romans 13:1-7, which we will identify with the call to do justice, and Matthew 5:21-48, the call to a life of *agape* (unconditional, suffering love of the other), as representative of two conflicting texts and see how different historical traditions have tried to resolve the conflict. (In this chapter, I will not be dealing with holy war texts, even though a case could be made for their use in Christian liberation movements.)

One approach that could be taken does not try to harmonize these conflicting texts but simply dismisses the nonresistant teachings of Jesus (as on the Sermon on the Mount) as meant for another time and place. This view sees the Matthew 5 teachings as having no bearing on contemporary political life, including modern warfare. John Howard Yoder, in *The Politics of Jesus*, maintains that mainstream social ethics presupposes that Jesus' hard teachings are not relevant for the complex realities of contemporary society and institutional life, while Paul's more conservative-sounding teachings on submission to God-given authority, even the use of the sword, seem to be more applicable.

Yoder rejects the notion that Jesus' teachings are irrelevant to the current situation and offers an alternative interpretation, one which he calls "biblical realism." In this interpretation, Jesus' teachings are imperative for Christian ethics and meant to be followed by Christians. Jesus, says Yoder, presents us with "one particular social-political-ethical option," a nonviolent, way-of-the cross approach to human relations in contemporary society.

Even if one accepts the social and political relevance of the Sermon on the Mount, one is still left with the problem of the conflicting texts. The question remains: how exactly is Jesus' teaching about "loving the enemy" and "turning the other cheek" to be interpreted and applied to complex contemporary societies in which violence is a fact of life? In *The Christian Witness to the State*, Yoder gives us seven ways in which resolutions of competing texts have been attempted. He does so by looking at seven Christian traditions, along with his own proposal, from the perspective of two New Testament streams: (1) Jesus' unconditional love ethic (*agape*), which calls for infinite forgiveness (Matthew 5); and (2) Natural law or justice, which is accessible to anyone aside from revelation (Romans 13). In the Old Testament, justice meant "eye for an eye," and in the New Testament this justice takes the form of Paul's injunctions in Romans 13. For the sake of brevity I will use Matthew 5 and Romans 13 to represent these two seemingly contradictory streams of thought.

(1) *Medieval Roman Catholic view.* In this reading, Matthew 5 sets out the councils of perfection meant for specially-called Religious Orders, and Romans 13 is intended for all others. This duality, in other words, is one of vocation. The two norms (*agape* love and justice) are both valid. But nonresistant love is determinative for people who are specially called to a more disciplined life of discipleship, while the justice ethic applies to the majority of people in public life. The latter is not strictly grounded in revelation but is found in the natural order, which is accessible to all, Christians and non-Christians alike. When applied to war and peace, one could say that the just war, with its rules of justice, applies to the world in general, particularly to those in positions of responsibility, while nonviolent love is expected of a minority of "religious," who are called out of society to live a more perfect life.

(2) *Traditional Lutheran view.* Here also there exists a duality, not between two groups of people, as in medieval Catholicism, but within each person—between inner disposition and personal relationships, on the one hand,

and public, vocational responsibilities, on the other. Each situation has to be examined separately to determine which norm applies. Nonviolent and nonresistant love applies to the personal sphere, and the use of force is brought to bear in the public sphere to maintain justice, law, and order. This dichotomy has sometimes been referred to as the two-kingdoms doctrine: one kingdom is the heavenly, inner realm of love, mercy, justifying grace, and the individual before God (Matthew 5); the other is the earthly, external kingdom of law and justice (Romans 13). In this two-kingdom view one can be a soldier going to war on behalf of the state, and a loving, nonviolent Christian following Jesus at the same time.

(3) *Classical Calvinist view*. This position is not a strictly dualistic view—Calvin, as we shall see in a later chapter, espoused a softer form of dualism between the inner and outer kingdoms—but one that draws ethical criteria not primarily from Matthew 5 or Romans 13 but from the whole Bible. Old Testament and New Testament are on an equal level in providing norms for moral and ethical behavior. Reason and nature do not give us different ethical norms from those of the Bible. The general norm for behavior is above eye-for-eye justice but below the nonresistant love of Matthew 5. Our actions oscillate between achieving more

than justice alone and less than perfect love. The Calvinist/Reformed tradition carries a great sense of responsibility for public life and the civil order. Although Calvin might be placed within the just war tradition, there are elements in his and later Reformed thought that have holy war motifs.

(4) *Liberal Pacifism.* The social ethics of liberalism is nondualistic in that it sees love as the norm for all, individuals and societies. The nature of this love is sometimes "unretaliating forgiveness" (the *agape* of Matthew 5), sometimes a lesser form of love akin to "redemptive justice." Love and justice are identified as a universal standard but are situationally relative. This movement assumes a general optimism, which reached its peak in the nineteenth century, that through rational discussion and education the world can be lifted to a higher moral level, one in which political conflicts could be resolved through nonviolent love rather than war. With the coming of the total wars of the twentieth century, this optimism has largely come to an end.

(5) *Christian Realism.* Reinhold Niebuhr, the most influential American ethicist of the twentieth century, represents a way of trying to bring together the nonviolent ideal of Jesus' teachings in Matthew 5 with the realism of relative justice found in Romans 13.

Niebuhr began as a theological and ethical liberal and gradually moved into what he called a Christian Realist approach, which maintained some aspects of his former liberalism, namely, the notion of love as the ideal under which all forms of justice need to be evaluated. His move away from liberalism came with his increasing pessimism about human nature and his conviction that the sinfulness (selfishness) of human beings makes any absolute application of the love ethic to society unrealistic. Like Martin Luther, Niebuhr believed that the individual Christian ought to decide on a case-by-case basis whether Matthew 5 (individual relations) or Romans 13 (public responsibilities) should apply. With the Catholics, Niebuhr believed that certain Greco-Roman ethical values can help guide the Christian's witness to and participation in the public realm. The "norm-lines" of justice as well as love are never fixed but relative to the situation. Justice in the real world is never absolute but always defined in terms of competing claims dragged downward by the fact of human fallenness and sin.

All the approaches above presuppose that Christian ethics apply to all of society. The views below could be described as "sectarian": they assume that Christian values of love and justice apply only to a faith community based on conversion and the imperative of Jesus' teachings. In these groups, a duality exists between the "church" (the Christian community), where belief in Christ is assumed, and the "world" (larger society), where such faith can not be presupposed.

(6) *Jehovah's Witnesses*. In the case of the Jehovah's Witnesses, the state is presumed to be diabolic and beyond theological norms, but occasionally it performs better than expected (e.g., when it does not persecute the faithful). The believing community for the Jehovah's Witnesses consists of an elect group of 144,000. For these the ethical norm is not the *agape* of Christ but the laws of the Old and New Testaments. The Jehovah's Witnesses have been one of the most persecuted minority groups in the West for their refusal to compromise their pacifism, especially during the National Socialist period in Germany.

(7) *Old Order Mennonites and Amish*. In these traditional groups, to be distinguished from the majority "mainstream" Mennonites, there is a duality between the Christian community of belief and the larger society, which is the realm of unbelief or other forms of belief. Unlike the Jehovah's Witnesses, traditional Amish and Mennonites do expect certain standards of the world, but these are lower than the agape of Jesus. The norms of

the state and its laws are closer to an eye-for-an-eye justice (as in capital punishment); the church lives by the norm of love and thus refuses to participate in political life and the armed forces. Sometimes the state rises above retributive justice and the state of war, but the standards of the world are independent of the perfection of Christ as found in Matthew 5.

8) *Yoder's Pacifism.* In his own proposal John Howard Yoder makes four assumptions: (a) The norm of the nonviolent love of Jesus is the only one that applies to the Christian church; (b) there is a duality between Christians and non-Christians; (c) the expectations of the world are less than the expectations of Christ's love; (d) nevertheless, love is a "relevant historical possibility." Yoder agrees with traditional sectarianism in the distinction between the realm of faith (the Christian community) and realm where faith in Christ cannot be assumed (larger society, the "world"). However, for him there is no absolute standard of justice for the world other than the imperative of love—there is no "norm willed by God other than love itself." Sin is the factor which keeps the world from performing according to the demands of love. The church witnesses to the world/state in two ways: It speaks to society using "middle axioms": norms the world can understand, such

as liberty, equality, democracy, and human rights. For believers these middle axioms are informed by Christ's norm of love, but they communicate to the world in its own language. The church also seeks to bring individuals from the world (including leaders) into the realm of faith ("conversion").

Conclusion

We have looked at numerous ways in which theological and church traditions have sought to resolve seemingly conflicting texts in the New Testament, using the contrasting passages of Matthew 5:38-48 and Romans 13:1-7 as examples. The former represents the "hard sayings" of Jesus, sometimes referred to as the "perfection of Christ" or the "councils of perfection." The latter is frequently used to justify a more conservative, "realistic" approach to the use of force in the punishment of evil and preservation of the good. In the former, the teachings of Jesus in the Sermon on the Mount do not make effectiveness the primary standard of ethical judgment but obedience to Jesus' example, with conversion as a prerequisite to a life of discipleship. Such ethics of discipleship cannot be imposed on society, even though the language of discipleship needs to be translated into terms that society can understand. It must be remembered that the rejection of violence is not a rejection of involvement in social transformation.

Critical for Christian social ethics, also in relation to violence and the use of force in maintaining public law and order, is to go beyond the Sermon on the Mount for ethical wisdom, to seek guidance from the whole Bible. I propose that the only way, ultimately, of reconciling the seemingly contradicting texts above is to read the Bible *theologically* from beginning to end (i.e., to seek the underlying pattern or trajectory) in order to discover the direction in which the drama of creation, sin/fall, redemption, and consummation is moving.

The various texts of the Bible, alongside the events of Christ's birth, life, teachings, death, resurrection and ascension, need to be placed into the context of the Trinitarian drama of God's own life. God the "Father" is the transcendent, mysterious, unbegotten origin of the created world who has power over life and death. God can in a mysterious way give and take life, turn evil into good, and even use violence to further the good. God the "Son" is the begotten of the Father who in his incarnation in Jesus as the Christ represents the way of nonviolent love as a means of reconciling the world through the cross, thereby revealing the "grain of the universe" (what God ultimately intends for the whole cosmos). As Christians we are called to follow by analogy this Jesus of Nazareth, the Christ, in how we live in the world. God the "Spirit" is the power of the resurrection by which a new humanity motivated by love can already in penultimate and fragmentary ways reflect the loving redemption of the world both inside and outside the Christian community.

4

Early Church:
Divided Evidence

Were the earliest Christians pacifists? Did they follow literally Jesus' call to love the enemy and turn the other cheek? Or were they opposed to Christian participation in the military for other reasons, such as idolatry? Although there is strong evidence that early Christians were pacifist until the second half of the second century and even beyond, this is not an indisputable fact. In this chapter we will survey the evidence, looking at both sides of the argument.

Evidence for Pacifism

First, we consider the case for the pacifism of the early church. There appears to be no official evidence of Christians in the army until about 170–180 of the Common Era (CE). We first hear, in 173 CE, of Marcus Aurelius's Christian militia called the Thundering Legion.

We have strong pacifist pronouncements from second- and third-century "Church Fathers": Justin Martyr, Clement of Alexandria, Origen, Tertullian, and Lactantius. There are church-related documents (for example, the Canons of Hippolytus, an order of discipline in effect from the early third into the fifth century) in which members of the church and baptismal candidates are forbidden to enter the army voluntarily and in which soldiers holding civil authority are instructed not to kill and to refuse to do so if commanded.

From this time we also have accounts of Christian martyrs who served in the military but refused to shed blood, suggesting that there were Christians in the army for civil services other than killing. We know that in the Roman Empire the military had a police function that included fire protection, care of prisoners, public transport, mail delivery, and secretarial work. All this evidence can be used to build a case for the refusal of early Christians to shed blood, even though some were in various forms of civil service under the authority of the government.

Evidence against Strict Pacifism

A strong case can be made against a strict pacifist reading of the early sources. There are ambiguous passages in the New Testament in which Christian converts who serve in civil and military positions, like the Centurian in Acts 10, are not told to give up their professions. The strong opposition by some of the church fathers, like Tertullian in the second century, to participation in the military suggests that there was a problem with Christians serving as soldiers, a divergence between the official position of the church and the actual practice in the churches. Tertullian's *Apology* (197 CE) assumes there are Christians in the palace, senate, forum, and army.

The fact that there were accounts of soldier martyrs demonstrates the presence of Christians in the army. Inscriptions and epitaphs in cemeteries show that soldiers were not denied burial in Christian graveyards. There appear to have been variations in practice according to territory; the Eastern frontier was more prone to having Christians in the army, anticipating by a century what would become common in the Constantinian period throughout the empire (as we shall see in the next chapter). We have mentioned the Thundering Legion of Christian soldiers under Aurelius in the second century. By 278 CE we read of Bishop Paul of Samosata having a Christian body guard.

Responding to Change

How is one to deal with the conflicting evidence and come to some satisfactory conclusion? The evidence, I propose, must be looked at in light of the theological-ethical choices the early Christian community had to make in the face of its changing situation in the Greco-Roman world. Theologians Hans Küng and David Tracy talk about "paradigm shifts" in Christian thought over the centuries. In the first few hundred years after Christ and the Apostles, a major paradigm shift took place in how earliest Christians saw themselves in relation to the world around them. Early Christians thought and lived within the "apocalyptic paradigm," assuming that the end of time, the kingdom of God, the *parousia* (second coming of Christ) was imminent.

Already in the later books of the New Testament one finds a change taking place, a realization that the church will be around for some time due to the delay of the *parousia*. Christians begin to make adjustments to the world and its institutions, which has implications for the church and its polity, especially the church's relation to the state and to society. Even developments in church dogma reflect this adjustment. One might say that the process of "Constantinianization," the alliance of church and state (which will be dealt with in the next chapter), begins at this early stage. The church gradually relaxes its opposition to the world due to a decrease in persecution.

At first there were no Christians in the army because it was not allowed by the church or the Roman state. Then some Christians were found in the army even though officially it was considered wrong. The second century Apologists (intellectual defenders of the faith) began using pagan (Greco-Roman) terms to communicate Christianity. The *Pax Romana* (Roman peace) was thought by some to be the beginning of the kingdom of God on earth, and the cultural and political border of the Roman Empire came to be accepted as worthy of defense by Christians. The church-world dualism that was so critical in the apocalyptic paradigm was now modified and transformed into a spirit-material dualism.

Four simultaneous developments reflect the change in attitude of the church to the surrounding culture: (1) *Canonization*, the collection and formation of the biblical writings, including both Jewish and Christian; (2) *Creedalization*, the writing of short doctrinal statements summarizing the Christian doctrine of God and related teachings; (3) *Institutionalization*, the creation of hierarchical church institutions considered necessary for stability and to preserve the faith from distortion; and (4) *Constantinianization*, the church becoming "establishment," allied with the state. The first three of these developments have a similar purpose: to preserve the apostolic message from heretical distortion.

With these developments also came a change in the church's attitude toward war and peace. Gradually, the church eased its strict prohibition against shedding blood. In the second and early third century, Tertullian (160–220 CE) and Origen (185–254 CE) were still strict pacifists, unequivocally forbidding Christians to serve in the army. There were at least two distinct schools of thought in early Christianity: the *Alexandrian*, which was more philosophical, Greek, and allegorical in its approach to interpreting scriptures, seeking to hold "Athens" (Greek philosophy) and "Jerusalem" (Jewish thought) together; and the *Antiochene*, which was more Jewish, historical, and literal in its hermeneutics, seeking to keep Jerusalem and Athens separate. Tertullian was Antiochene in approach, declaiming, "What has Jerusalem to do with Athens?" Origen was Alexandrian.

Tertullian, son of a pagan centurion, and later member of the rigorist, schismatic Montanist sect, wrote a number of works (*On the*

Crown, The Apology, On Idolatry) that are pacifist, anti-military books. He did not reject the Old Testament books, as did the heretical second-century Bishop Marcion, but he did believe the Old Testament had been superseded by the New. While he did not eschew philosophical reasoning, he felt it should be subordinated to the "Rule of Faith," the church's dogmatic teaching. The Old Testament should be read in the light of tradition. He was a pacifist but not a "sectarian pacifist" (he did not reject the concept of government and the state as such). His pacifism was based on more than just rejection of violence. His critique of the military was aimed against the military lifestyle, which included idolatry in its veneration of the Emperor, killing, and immorality. In his *On Idolatry*, Tertullian says the following:

> A dispute arose recently on this point. Can a servant of God undertake an administrative office or function if, by favor or ingenuity, he can keep himself clear of every form of idolatry . . . ? Grant that a man may succeed in holding his office, whatever it may be, quite nominally, never sacrifice, never authorize a sacrifice, never contract for sacrificial victims, never delegate the supervision of a temple, never handle their taxes,

never give a show at his own expense or the
State's, never even take an oath; and on top
of all that, in the exercise of his magisterial authority, never try anyone on a capital
charge or one involving loss of civil status
(you may tolerate inflicting a fine), never
condemn to death by verdict or legislation,
never put a man in irons or in prison, never
put to torture—well, if you think that is possible, he may hold his office.[1]

Origen, on the other hand, used an allegorical approach to interpreting scripture, sub-
ordinating the literal meaning to spiritual
readings. This allowed him to hold together
violent Old Testament passages, on one side,
and gnostic Christianity, on the other. In his
important work on biblical interpretation, *On
First Principles*, he proposes a triple meaning
to scriptural texts: the literal interpretation
is analogous to the body, the moral reading
to the soul, and the mystical and theological reading to the spirit. Less separatist and
literal in his approach than Tertullian, Origen saw the Christian life as being fulfilled
gradually, part of the cosmic movement of
reunion with God enabled by the eternal
Logos, guided by the Holy Spirit. Like Tertullian, he did not deny the legitimacy of government but rejected Christian involvement

with professional military violence, based on an allegorical reading of violent passages in the Old Testament.

It is non-Christians, according to Origen, who are permitted involvement in necessary wars. He is less rigorous than Tertullian in adhering to the Sermon on the Mount because he recognizes the fallenness of the world and the difficulty of living according to Jesus' lofty ideals. Progress toward the kingdom of God is a gradual process. Here is what Origen says: "For we no longer take up 'sword against nation' nor do we 'learn war anymore,' having become children of peace, for the sake of Jesus, who is our leader, instead of those whom our fathers followed."[2] Origen also says: "Thus it will be neither lawful for a just man to engage in warfare, since his warfare is justice itself, no difference whether you put a man to death by word, or rather by the sword, since it is the act of putting to death itself which is prohibited."[3] Rather, Christians form a special army of piety and, as such, provide a greater service to society by praying for the king and keeping their hands pure.

This strong witness against Christians being in the military—on grounds of the army's un-Christian and idolatrous lifestyle, and its shedding of blood—was gradually relaxed in the third, fourth, and fifth centuries as the church made its peace with surrounding culture and the state. Even the Constantinian adjustment in the fourth century, at least partially a result of the success of the missionary movement, was met with considerable resistance by many Christians, such as monastics, and accepted with an uneasy conscience by others.

What we see in this Patristic period, the era of the church fathers, is the church coming to terms with its changing relationship to Greco-Roman culture. Church leaders are concerned with the development of dogma, formulating doctrines of the Trinity and of Christology, and with social ethics, such as Christian participation in the military. One can see here the ongoing development of a pacifist ethic as well as increasing involvement of Christians in the ambiguities of civil and imperial life.

5

Constantinian Shift: The Justifiable War

A gradual shift in how Christians viewed their relationship to society took place in the first few centuries after Christ, as noted in the previous chapter. The earliest Christians viewed the times apocalyptically—they thought that the end of time and history was imminent. By the second century, this apocalyptic paradigm was being replaced with what Hans Küng calls the "orthodox" paradigm, a period in which the major creeds and confessions were formulated, based on "the rule of faith." This was an attempt to safeguard the Christian message from distortion by two extremes: the overly materialistic interpretation of the Ebionites, who emphasized the humanity of Jesus, and the overly spiritualistic interpretation of the Docetists, who emphasized the divine character of Christ.

It became ever more clear to the early Christians that the return of Christ at the end of time had been delayed and that they would have to come to terms with their social, economic, political, and religious environment. This, combined with the success of the missionary movement beginning with the Apostle Paul's mission to the Gentiles, meant that more and more pagans, even high-ranking officials and their spouses, were converting to Christianity. This meant that the moral and ethical attitudes of Christians began to reflect a new sense of responsibility for the social order, including the civil and military service.

The symbol of this turn is the conversion of Emperor Constantine the Great in the early fourth century. The shift that had been gradually occurring ever since the second century now became more pronounced. The changing attitude of the church to the use of force and warfare is most dramatically illustrated by the development at this time of the "just" or "justifiable" war. Although just war thinking began earlier, it is during the fourth century that the outline of the doctrine of the just war started to take shape.

The Constantinian watershed can be interpreted *positively* as the great finale of a successful missionary effort. Christian values now permeated and transformed the Roman Empire, and civil laws were grounded not on polytheistic beliefs but on Christian divine law.

Or the great Constantinian shift can be viewed *negatively* as an erosion of early Christianity, an erosion that began shortly after the death of the first apostles and gathered momentum in the work of the second-century Apologists, such as Justin Martyr.

These Apologists, particularly the Alexandrian school of theologians, combined Greek philosophical thought and Judeo-Christian theology in order to bring greater clarity to central theological doctrines, such as developing a Christian doctrine of God as triune, and to convince the pagan world of the truth of Christianity. In their apologetic work they assumed a common, foundational rationality between classical philosophy and Christian revelation. This made it possible to argue, as did Justin Martyr, that Plato had received his ideas from the Hebrews and that, truth being truth no matter where it is found, the great Greek philosophers must have been Christian before Christ. Similarly, there was a development of social ethics that took Christian responsibility within the Greco-Roman culture seriously. Arguments for such responsibility were increasingly based on philosophy and natural law (reason) in addition to, or even in place of, biblical revelation, such as the teachings of Jesus.

Constantine's "Conversion"

Up to the third century, the Roman Empire was strong, stable, orderly, and prosperous. In the third century, power shifted away from the Roman senate to the military as the empire was threatened by barbarian invasions, civil war, and chaos. Militarism eclipsed all intellectual, cultural, and political life. It was under these conditions of threat to the empire from within and without and growing militarism that Constantine came to power. It is in this light that his conversion and policies, especially in regard to the religions of the empire, must be appraised. In 312, Constantine moved against Maxentius's army in Italy—Maxentius had laid claim to the western half of the empire. The night before this definitive battle against Maxentius, at the Milvian Bridge on the Tiber River, Constantine supposedly had his famous vision. This vision and his subsequent victory became the basis of his "conversion" to Christianity.

What was said to have happened at that moment in history was the fateful identification of "cross" and "sword." There are a number of versions of what happened that night. But the most common account, according to Eusebius (a pro-Constantine theologian), is that Constantine "saw with his own eyes the trophy of a cross of light in the heavens, above the sun,

and bearing the inscription *Conquer by This.*"[1]
What follows is even more critical. Constantine described the vision to his army, and he had a new banner made for his soldiers to carry into battle, described thus by Eusebius: "A long spear, overlaid with gold, formed the figure of the cross by means of a traverse bar laid over it."[2] Whether historically accurate or not, this account is what shapes the subsequent ideological identification of Christian cross and imperial sword.

Already in 311, Constantine had issued an Edict of Toleration for different religions in his realm. Within a year after the Milvian Bridge battle, Constantine was in control of the western half of the empire. In 313, he and Licinius, the Augustus of the East, jointly declared the Edict of Milan, which gave religious freedom to Jews, Christians, and pagans in the empire. By 324, the year he called together the bishops for a conference at Nicaea, Constantine had defeated Licinius and gained control of the whole Roman Empire.

Herein lies the irony. Up to the time of Constantine, Christians were seen as a threat to polytheistic pluralism and tolerance in Roman society, partly due to their proselytizing, and so they were persecuted. With Constantine and the official recognition of Christianity, forces were set in motion that would eventually replace that pluralism and tolerance with a Christian hegemony or predominance, which resulted in the persecution of non-Christians. This Christian hegemony was achieved by the identification of cross and sword. Now it became legal to persecute pagans and Jews, as well as Christian heretics, such as Docetists, Donatists, Nestorians, and Arians.

Theologian Lactantius, personal adviser and tutor to Constantine and his son, envisioned a civil constitution based on Christian monotheism, with laws grounded in divine law. This was put into effect under Constantine, the first Christian emperor. The understanding of citizenship and one's duties to the state changed dramatically under Constantine. Whereas earlier citizens demonstrated their loyalty to the state by performing rituals of worship to the gods, now their loyalty was increasingly determined by their allegiance to the Christian God and the emperor. Prayer for the protection of Rome replaced sacrifice to the gods, and the protection of the new state involved the identification of Christ and sword.

Whatever good intentions Lactantius and Constantine may have had about not using violence or force in religious matters, when Christianity became the religious foundation of the the empire, military defense of "the homeland" became a moral obligation, particularly for Christians. This was evident in subsequent years as just war theory developed to justify Christian participation in the military under certain conditions. Persecution of Jews and heretics soon spread to other religions. Between 325 and 381, state and church became allies against the heretics. By 392, pagan temples were closed.

In 420, Augustine, the father of just war principles, gave his approval to coercive-repressive measures against Christian dissenters. Whereas Christians had earlier been excluded from the army, by 436 non-Christians were excluded. The shift was complete.

Development of Just War

This brings us to the development of the principles under which war might be justified. Despite its fragmented origins in the thought of Saint Ambrose (d. 397) and Saint Augustine (d. 430), just war thinking came over time to be the dominant position of the Roman Catholic Church as well as most mainline Protestant traditions, including Lutheran, Reformed, Anglican, and Presbyterian. Ambrose, Bishop of Milan, drew on Old Testament, New Testament, and Stoic sources to argue that conduct in war should be just and that priests should abstain.

Augustine, also drawing on Hebrew, Christian, and classical sources, proposed a bare outline of what later became the full-fledged set of just war criteria: just intention (to restore peace); just objective (vindicate justice); just disposition (love); just auspices (ruling authority); just conduct (no wanton violence); just discrimination (between combatants and non-combatants).

Important to remember is that Augustine differentiated between the City of God (heavenly city), which was characterized by love of God and neighbor, the ground for all genuine happiness and peace, and the City of Man (earthly city) governed by love of self, violence, and war. Augustine had a pessimistic view of human beings and of history, describing it as the arena for the conflict between these two loves (God and self). The earthly city, however, shares partially in heavenly peace when it properly orders relationships and the various levels of "the good."

For Augustine, civic authority, which is responsible for this ordering of relationships, depends on power and coercion as a necessary evil for waging war against evil. Because it contradicts the peace and love of the heavenly city, war is never a good; it is always a tragic necessity because human beings live in a fallen and sinful world. War can justifiably be fought only if certain conditions are met, as itemized above. War can be justified as an action on behalf of a third party, which can be reconciled with Christ's call to love of neighbor, never in self-defense. Later in life, Augustine compromised his earlier rigorous ethic by justifying the use of force against "heretics" (such as the Donatists), thereby nearly collapsing the ideal and the real within the Christian community.

In time, just war theory or, more accurately, the justifiable war tradition, developed standard criteria, although there is no absolute list of such criteria. These are normally divided into conditions leading up to war (*jus ad bellum*), and those relevant for the actual conduct of war (*jus in bello*). The criteria usually associated with the first are: (1) legitimate authority declaring and waging war; (2) just cause; (3) peace as the ultimate intention or goal; (4) love of neighbor, not hatred or vengefulness, as the motivation; (5) war as last resort—all other avenues must have been exhausted before going to war; and (6) probability of success.

The four criteria usually identified with just conduct in war are: (7) means as commensurate with the intended end; (8) proportionality of means to end—the harm caused must not exceed the harm prevented; (9) immunity of innocent people—the distinction between combatants and noncombatants; and (10) respect for international law.³ While there is general agreement that some rational criteria for limiting war are better than none, there is serious disagreement on whether these criteria have ever been successfully applied to a war when national interest is at stake.

Changing Assumptions

In concluding this chapter, we should note that in the transition from the early Christian apocalyptic worldview to the Constantinian paradigm there were some fundamental shifts in how Christians viewed their relationship to the surrounding society. First, there was a shift in the understanding of God's providence: earlier, God was thought to be visibly present in the church and invisibly present in society and the actions of the state; later thinking saw God visibly present in the politics of the empire and in a sense invisibly present in the church. Augustine, for example, saw the church as a "mixed body" of believers and unbelievers that would be sorted out only at the end of time.

Second, there was a transition in moral and ethical reasoning. Whereas earlier the norms for ethics were biblical revelation (Moses and Jesus), with Constantine came reliance on common sense and natural law, norms that could be applied to the running of an empire. Third, there was a move from the duality of Christian and world to a Platonic duality of spirit and matter. Christianity became a religion that holds society together and gives it unity.

In my own tradition (Anabaptist-Mennonite), along with other groups in the Free Church or Believer's Church traditions, "Constantinianism" has become a shibboleth or catch-all for everything that is wrong with mainstream Christianity, including its stance toward war and peace. While I find myself in considerable agreement with the critique of the so-called Constantinian compromise, especially as it applies to the use of force and violence, I have in my own work sought to analyze in a more differentiated way the Constantinian problem.

I would argue that the Constantinian period is much more diverse than often acknowledged, and the Constantinian dilemma—whether to remain uncompromisingly faithful to Jesus' teaching of nonresistant love or to draw on extra-Christological criteria for involvement in society—cannot be avoided wherever Christianity is engaged in mission and confronts wider culture.

6

Middle Ages:
From Just War to Crusade

In the previous chapter we considered the rise of the "justifiable war" in the context of the first Christian emperor, Constantine the Great. In this chapter we look at the career of the just war in the medieval period, from the fifth to sixteenth centuries. We will also trace the emergence of the Crusades and the minority witness to pacifism.

The breakup of the Roman Empire in the West after the fifth century profoundly affected the rules and application of the just war. Medieval Europe was now divided into many small feudal fiefdoms, all under the overarching embrace of the Roman Catholic Church, and later under the Holy Roman Empire. The eleventh to thirteenth centuries saw the rise of the Crusades or holy war against the "infidels" of the East.

Changes in Just War Thinking

Just war thinking underwent significant changes during the Middle Ages. First of all, the breakup of the empire into many units, with feuding princes defending their own territories, complicated the issue of legitimate authority under which war could be fought. The clashes between church and Holy Roman Empire facilitated the rise of city-states and nation-states, which brought further ambiguities not covered adequately by early just war rules as envisioned by Augustine.

Second, Christianity became militarized, especially by "Germanic tribes," even though the number of people involved in military forces remained comparatively small: the prince, knights of various kinds, and mercenaries. Mercenaries, of course, were concerned primarily with a salary and their own survival, not which side was right or wrong. Ordinary citizens were not considered suitable for the military; they were without skill and weaponry.

Third, the distinction between laity and clergy became blurred as bishops became princes, or counselors to princes and kings, becoming deeply embroiled in politics. The social hierarchies were such that the question of who could legitimately conduct war against whom was increasingly ambiguous, calling into question the just war presupposition that war is fought between equals within an overarching unity such as empire.

Fourth, the shift from an urban society to an agrarian one also had an impact on just war criteria, as the defense of private property became important. Fifth, the emergence of the notion of the "individual conscience," already evident in the writings of Thomas Aquinas, now became a factor in resisting or supporting a war. Sixth, the development of sacramental theology brought with it an increasing concern for sacramental purity; clergy were exempted from fighting on sacramental rather than purely ethical grounds.

Seventh, just war criteria came to be applied in the realm of canon law and confessional requirements: "The criteria became operative when the question arose as to whether a knight returning from battle could be permitted to receive the Eucharist, and what difference it made in that connection whether the war was just or not. Even for killing in a *just* cause some period of penance was demanded. Even for killing in a *just* cause a candidate for the priesthood could be rendered incapable of receiving orders."[1]

Eighth, a number of developments connected with the Cluniac Reforms of the eleventh century had the effect of tempering the militarism of the Middle Ages. One of the reforms, "The Peace of God," declared that certain places were off-limits to fighting (such as places of sanctuary and refuge), and certain persons were exempted from warfare (clergy, religious, penitents, peasants, etc.). "The Truce of God" limited the times in which fighting could occur (not in Advent, Lent, or other holy days and feast days). This meant that the church represented a limiting influence over war and violence.

Ninth, the church in the thirteenth and fourteenth centuries, through the mediating efforts of bishops, kings, and nobles, was involved in arbitration and peacemaking between warring factions. Tenth, the church inaugurated various peace liturgies (peace masses, celebrations at the end of war, peacemaking saints) to emphasize the significance of peace efforts. Finally, the church had the power of sanction, the most extreme form being excommunication, as a way of enforcing the above restraints.

Thomas Aquinas

Thomas Aquinas clearly presented this medieval understanding of the just war in the four articles making up Question 40 ("Of War") of his *Summa Theologica* II-II. In Article One, drawing on biblical sources (such as Romans 13:4) and Augustine, Aquinas identifies three conditions necessary for a just war. First, war must be waged by a just authority or sovereign, not by private individuals. Second, there must be a just cause, some fault on the part of those attacked (like avenging a wrong or restoration of what has been unjustly seized). Third, war must be fought with right intention: the advancement of the good, avoidance of evil, securing peace, punishing evil-doers, rather than cruelty or aggrandizement.

In Article Two, Aquinas argues that different things are required from different persons for the sake of the common good. Clerics and bishops must not fight for two reasons: (1) "warlike pursuits are full of unrest, so that they hinder the mind very much from the contemplation of Divine things, the praise of God, and prayers for the people, which belong to the duties of a cleric";

> (2) all the clerical Orders are directed to the ministry of the altar, on which the Passion of Christ is represented sacramentally. . . . Wherefore it is unbecoming for them to slay or shed blood, and it is more fitting that they should be ready to shed their own blood for Christ, so as to imitate in deed what they

portray in their ministry. . . . Wherefore it is altogether unlawful for clerics to fight, because war is directed to the shedding of blood.

In Article Four, Aquinas conditionally allows for fighting on holy days: "Therefore, for the purpose of safeguarding the common weal of the faithful, it is lawful to carry on a war on holy days, provided there be need for doing so: because it would be to tempt God, if not withstanding such a need, one were to choose to refrain from fighting."

In Article One of Question 41 ("Of Strife"), Aquinas allows in some circumstances for self-defense in what he calls personal warfare:

But in him who defends himself, it may be without sin, or it may sometimes involve a venial sin, or sometimes a mortal sin; and this depends on his intention and on his manner of defending himself. For if his sole intention be to withstand the injury done to him, and he defend himself with due moderation, it is no sin, and one cannot say properly that there is strife on his part. But if, on the other hand, his self-defense be inspired by vengeance and hatred, it is always a sin . . . it is a mortal sin if he makes for his assailant with the fixed intention of killing him, or inflicting grievous harm on him.

Richard B. Miller has argued persuasively that in Aquinas's articulation of the just war there is a strong presumption against harming others (loving the neighbor) that can occasionally be overridden for the sake of higher priorities, such as protecting the common good: "Sometimes those requirements [neighbor love] may be overridden by weightier considerations, like the protection of the commonweal. A presumption in favour of nonresistance ought to order the Christian's 'attitude of mind,' which on occasion may be outweighed by considerations of communal protection. In this way, the justice of war is a function of ranking competing duties."[2]

The Crusades

Just war restraints were removed in the Crusades against the so-called infidels in the East. In the late eleventh century, the Turks advanced toward and threatened the Christian government in Byzantium. In 1095, Alexius Comenus, who had seized the Eastern throne in 1081, appealed to Western Christendom through Pope Urban II for military aid to fight the Turks who were in control of Asia Minor. The Pope was impressed by the urgency of the request from Byzantium, even though for decades the papacy had been uneasy with Eastern patriarchs. Also, the Pope saw this as an opportunity to achieve peace in the West, where there had been internecine strife between the papacy and the Holy Roman Empire for decades.

The Pope decided to use the occasion of the Council of Claremont, which had opened on November 18, 1095, to make an appeal for the first Crusade to the East. On November 27, 1095, he addressed a gathering of both clergy and laity announcing his plan to organize an army to go to the East to liberate the lands from the Turkish enemy.

What Urban II in effect initiated was a holy war against the Muslim Turks. In his appeal he called on the warring parties in the West to stop their intramural squabbles and to focus their attention abroad: "Let this mutual hatred stop; let these quarrels abate; let these wars cease; and let all these conflicts and controversies be put to rest. Begin the journey to the Holy Sepulcher; conquer that land which the wicked have seized, the land which was given by God to the children of Israel and which, as the Scripture says, is all milk and honey." He continues: "Undertake this journey, therefore, for the remission of your sins, with the assurance of 'glory which cannot fade' in the kingdom of heaven."[3]

His audience is said to have shouted "God wills it! God wills it!" and Urban is to have replied, "I tell you, therefore, that God placed this shout in your breasts and that God brought it out. Since this shout came from God, let it be your battle cry. When you make an armed attack on the enemy, let all those on God's side cry out together, 'God wills it! God wills it!'"[4] Like so often in the history of war, the battle against an external enemy is a way of solving domestic problems. Just War at home, Crusade abroad!

The trek to the East was seen by many as a holy pilgrimage, a sacred sacrifice in which participants were to wear the sign of the cross in obedience to the Lord's command: "Whoever does not take up the cross and follow me is not worthy of me" (Matthew 10:38). Here the early church's teaching to take up the self-sacrificial cross rather than to take another's life was reversed: Crusaders were now called to take up the cross as a sword to kill others. In the second Crusade, proclaimed on December 1, 1145, by Eugene III, Abbot Bernard of Clairvaux preached powerful sermons on behalf of the Crusade to the French King Louis VII's court during the Easter season. Saint Bernard became, in fact, "the official preacher and the guiding spirit of the Second Crusade."[5]

The monastic movement, which in the fourth century had represented a nonviolent protest against the Constantinian shift, now in Saint Bernard became an advocate of imperial wars against the infidel. We see a dramatic change from the earlier pacifist and just war approaches to the violence of the Holy Crusade, supported by the most religious in society. According to Roland Bainton, "The code of the just war which was being elaborated and refined by the secular ideals of chivalry and the church's ideal of the Truce and Peace of God, was largely in abeyance in fighting the infidel. Crucifixion, ripping open those who had swallowed coins, mutilation—Behemond of Antioch sent to the Greek Emperor a whole cargo of noses and thumbs sliced from the Saracens—such exploits the chronicles of the crusades recount without qualm."[6] Monastic orders such as the Templars and Order of Saint John (Knights Hospitaller), originally charged with caring for wounded soldiers, soon became militant and joined the fighting.

Although initially conceived as a holy pilgrimage to the East, inspired by the peacemaking aims of the Cluniac reforms, the Crusades turned into a religious war against the infidel that did not meet the standards of the just war.

The leaders of the Crusade . . . were men with very mixed motives and ideals. . . . The Crusaders were enthusiastic, but they had not yet created a clear ideology that all the soldiers in the army could share. The common soldiers had very different hopes and ideals. Some saw a new world and some would have been attracted by the lure of the Holy City of Jerusalem. Many may have believed that they would improve their lot and become rich and famous or they might simply have wanted an adventure, as well as having a strong piety. But all these mixed motives were transformed by the experience of the Crusade itself. Crusading turned out to be quite different from what anybody had expected and the terror and wonder of the campaign gave birth to an ideal of a distinctively Christian version of the holy war.[7]

And when these armies of soldiers, clerics, and peasants returned home, they were employed to fight heretics and dissidents at home under the umbrella of the Inquisition, which was founded in the twelfth century.

Pacifist Movements Continue

Despite the crusading mentality of the times, anti-war and pacifist movements continued as a minority current throughout the Middle Ages. Alongside the evolution of the just war doctrine, and the triumphant militarism of the Crusades, there existed small groups of Christians who refused to join military movements and the call to war. Monastic orders such as the Franciscans and sectarian groups such as the Cathars, the Waldensians, and the Hussites rejected violence and warfare.

The Hussite leader, Peter Chelciky, anticipated many of the ideas of later pacifist sects which emerged during the Reformation. He believed "that the first age of the Church was the golden age and this age was pacifist; that Christ's law was the law of love which forbids killing; and that his weapon was spiritual only and his mission to redeem souls, not to destroy bodies. The fall of the Church began with Constantine with the union of Church and state."[8]

Pacifistic currents were also evident in Aquinas's exemption of clergy from the shedding of blood on sacramental grounds, and in the "Peace of God" and "Truce of God" prescriptions in the Cluniac Reforms. All of these bore witness to a radical option for Christians: Jesus' way of nonviolent love. While these movements were in the minority, the witness to Christ's nonviolent way of the cross was never lost in the church.

7

Reformation:
The Magisterial Reformers

The "Magisterial" Reformers are those who, in the early sixteenth century, called for the reform of the church and the state and allied themselves with rulers (magistrates) to help bring about change. These were the Lutherans or "Evangelical" churches (not to be confused with American evangelicalism), and the Reformed or Calvinist groups with roots in the thought of Ulrich Zwingli and John Calvin.

The sixteenth-century Reformation began to see the collapse of the medieval synthesis of church and state, with new understandings emerging about the relationship between them. The notion of a grand synthesis of religion and society (known as "Christendom") now gradually gave way to a two-kingdom theology in which church and state had their autonomous spheres of responsibility. Initially, this two-kingdom theology was especially true for Lutherans, and less so for Calvinists. It became even more central for the Radical Reformers, as we shall see in the next chapter.

Both the just war tradition, which emerged in the Constantinian period of the fourth century, and the crusade or holy war of the eleventh to thirteenth centuries presupposed that the church was actively involved in affairs of state and society, that it had responsibility for history and the larger world. Just war thought, which developed further in the medieval period, was never completely replaced by the crusade mentality driven by the fight against infidels or outsiders.

Although the dominant position of both Lutherans and Calvinists was an adapted version of the just war—certain conditions had to be met to make war legitimate—the rise of regional nationalisms added new criteria to just war thinking, such as national defense and assertion of national identity. These could take on holy war characteristics, as they did in the Peasants War of the early sixteenth century and the devastating Religious Wars of the post-Reformation period (up to the middle of the seventeenth century).

Tridentine Catholicism (named after the Council of Trent in the mid-sixteenth century), under the imperial banner of the Holy

Roman Emperor Charles V together with papal power, continued to justify war on Thomistic just war grounds (those outlined by Thomas Aquinas). Lutherans adapted the just war criteria to accommodate the demands of a growing number of new German princes who were seeking autonomy from imperial and papal authority. Sociologically, it could be argued that Roman Catholicism sided with the old aristocratic and imperial forces, Lutheranism with the growing number of new princes who were restless for greater autonomy from Rome and empire, and Calvinism with the growing middle classes, urban merchants, and bourgeoisie. The Radical Reformers sided primarily with the peasants and artisans. On a personal level, increasing importance was being given to individual conscience, reason, and experience.

Luther and the Two Kingdoms

Martin Luther encouraged the princes to put down and slaughter the rebellious peasants. In his 1526 essay, "Whether Soldiers, Too, Can be Saved," Luther identifies three types of war: (1) among equals, (2) overlord against subject, and (3) subject against overlord. Only the first two can be defended, he said. A revolt by a subject against an overlord is never justified.

To start a war is always wrong. Only a defensive, reactive, or necessary war is justified.

Luther is socially conservative and believes
in an organic, hierarchical society structured
in the following order of importance: God,
emperor, prince, count, noble, judge, peasant. All persons under God have an authority above them and an inferior below who is
subject to them. God deals with the nobility,
and the nobles with the peasants; the peasants have their own family hierarchy: men,
women, children, pets. Violence is allowable
only between equals or against those beneath
one. The responsibility of princes and nobles
is to protect and defend those in their juris-
diction, except when they revolt. The Christian attitude in war is to submit one's body
and soul to God, draw one's sword, and fight
in the name of God.

Luther's whole position on war is grounded
in his understanding of the "two kingdoms,"
which correspond to two types of government:
(1) the heavenly, inner or spiritual kingdom,
which is governed by faith, love, nonresistance,
and justification by grace; and (2) the temporal
or earthly kingdom, which is governed by law,
order, and force. Although all Christians live
in both realms—one private, the other public—
the two ought never to be confused. Temporal
authority, according to Romans 13:1-4 and

1 Peter 2:13-14, is divinely instituted to punish the wicked and protect the good. Where the heavenly kingdom is concerned, Christians do not defend themselves but turn the other cheek; in the earthly realm, they are called to be strong and even brutal, especially in situations where they are vocationally responsible for others. A Christian therefore should be an especially good soldier or hangman. Soldiers, of course, are saved not by being good soldiers but by being justified by grace through faith.

The traditional Lutheran approach to war and violence that I have outlined here reflects its conservative, hierarchical context and should not be applied without qualification to later forms of Lutheranism. The Lutheran church's approach to war could take extreme nationalistic turns, as in the period of German National Socialism in the twentieth century. Theologians such as Emanuel Hirsch, for example, explicitly used Luther's two-kingdom teaching to support the pro-Hitler German Christians.[1] But there are also numerous counter examples of Lutheran Christians who defied the Nazis, such as members of the Resistance, the Pastors' Emergency League, and the Confessing Church. Dietrich Bonhoeffer and Paul Tillich, theologians who strongly resisted National Socialism, were committed to Lutheran thought and strongly advocated for peace and social justice

at the same time. Bonhoeffer went so far as
to espouse a form of pacifism in some of his
writings.

Calvin and Civil Government

John Calvin in his *Institutes of the Christian
Religion* also adheres to a notion of the two
kingdoms: (1) an inward kingdom that relates
to eternal life, and (2) an external one that
pertains to civil institutions and regulation of
behavior. However, where Luther is adamant
that the two realms should not tell each other
what to do, Calvin believes that the spiritual
kingdom as represented by the church has a
responsibility to tell temporal rulers what to
do, and temporal rulers have a right to regu-
late the external order or polity of the church.

Calvin's strict ordering of the behavior of Christians in Geneva according to biblical laws has
sometimes been called a theocracy—government
based on divine law(s). The internal, says Calvin,
"begins the heavenly kingdom in us," and the
external "is assigned, so long as we live among
men, to foster and maintain the external worship of God, to defend sound doctrine and the
condition of the church, to adapt our conduct to
human society, to form our manners to civil justice,
to conciliate us to each other, to cherish common peace and tranquillity."[2]

Relying extensively on Old Testament texts for his argument, he claims that magistrates are invested with divine authority representing the person of God; they are vice-regents of God (Jeremiah 22:3). In meting out punishment, the magistrate is not acting on behalf of the state alone but is executing the very judgment of God. The three types of law for Calvin are moral, ceremonial, and judicial, and the aim and end of all law is equity. Parting company with Luther, who would never countenance the rebellion of an inferior against a superior, Calvin allows for the exceptional case. While even magistrates of the worst type are to be esteemed, there is a point where God raises "avengers appointed to curb the tyranny of kings."

Calvin also discusses whether war is lawful and whether the New Testament teaches against its lawfulness. Kings and states, he says, have been given the power and responsibility to repress seditious movements, assist the violently oppressed, punish crimes, and generally to maintain the tranquility of their subjects. They are the guardians of the laws and must repress all criminal conduct that threatens those laws. It makes no difference whether it is the king or the lowliest subject, any who infringe on a territory that is not under their authority must be punished like a robber. "Natural equity and duty . . . demand that princes be armed not only to repress private crimes by judicial inflictions, but to defend the subjects committed to their guardianship whenever they are hostilely assailed."[3]

In many passages of scripture, according to Calvin, the Holy Spirit declares the use of such force to be lawful. What about the objection that in the New Testament one finds no teaching that war is lawful? Calvin responds that: (1) the ancient reasons for conducting war are still valid, (2) one ought not search the Apostolic writings for guidance in these matters, for their purpose was to establish the spiritual kingdom of Christ, not to form a civil society, and (3) Christ made no change in these matters, for he told those who were involved in civil matters to be content with their pay, not to quit their jobs.

Calvin then proceeds to defend the classical rules of the just war: magistrates should not give way to their passions or conduct themselves with anger and "implacable severity" but show pity to the offender as one having a common nature; they should not take up arms except when "compelled by the strongest necessity"—all other means must be tried before having recourse to arms; the sole regard must be for the public good. The power of the magistrates has been given for service

to others and includes the right to wage war
on behalf of those in their power.

Calvinism Radicalized

Calvin's arguments were radicalized a short
time later by French Calvinist Philip Mornay in his 1579 essay "A Defense of Liberty
against Tyrants." Writing some five years
after the infamous slaughter of the French
Protestants, the Huguenots, in the Saint Bar-
tholomew massacre, Mornay argues against
those who think the church should not defend
itself with arms because of the teaching and
example of Jesus Christ. The Apostle Paul
contradicts such pacifist notions in Romans
13, which exhorts Christians to be subject
to higher powers for they are ordained by
God. Also, Christ granted the centurion his
request without asking him to quit his post,
John the Baptist commanded men at arms to
be content with their pay, and Peter baptized
Cornelius, a centurion.

Military captains, centurions, and men at
arms were always received into the church,
argues Mornay. The early church had legions
of Christian soldiers, and there were those in
the army who suffered martyrdom for confessing the name of Christ. Under Constantine, it
was considered lawful to make war to preserve

towns in the empire and repulse an invading enemy. In the Crusades, Christian princes fought against the Turks and Saracens to conquer the Holy Land for Christianity.

Mornay argues further that if it is lawful to bear arms and to make war, then what could be more just than to defend the church and preserve the faithful? The church may not be increased by arms but may be preserved by them. In fact, those responsible for a town draw upon themselves the judgment of God if they do not by all their means attempt to protect their own. Such war ought, however, not to be fought by private persons. Is it lawful then, asks Mornay, to resist tyranny, to overthrow a prince who oppresses the people in his realm? One can use rationally grounded natural law to distinguish between a good and a bad prince. God elects kings, and people establish kings—throughout the Old Testament and throughout history one can see that the legitimacy of rulers comes from the people. Therefore it is legitimate for people to overthrow an oppressive government.

Parting company with the hierarchical views of Luther and the Catholic tradition of his time, Mornay maintains that the true sovereignty of kings in the Old Testament lies in the entire congregation, the assembly. The king emerges from the people, and the assembly of the people is above the king, although where this body is too large it may be represented by officers. So in Mornay we see the development of the republican spirit that later is embodied in the Cromwellian revolution in England and in American revolutionary Puritanism.

8

Radical Reformation:
From Revolution to Pacifism

The Radical Reformation has left us a rich and varied heritage of reflection on war and peace. The Mennonites, descendents of the Radical Reformers or Anabaptists, have in their five-hundred-year history come to be identified with sectarian pacifism and non-resistance. However, their origins in the "left wing" of the sixteenth-century Reformation reveal a considerable diversity on such issues as the relation of church to world, and the use of violence. Historians such as Hans-Jürgen Goertz, James Stayer, and Werner Packull have traced the "polygenetic" origins of first-generation Anabaptism and have shown the close relationship between early Anabaptist radicals, such as Hans Hut and Balthasar Hubmaier, and the peasant revolts of the 1520s.

The apocalyptic rhetoric of Hut and Thomas Müntzer, who greatly influenced Anabaptists, had much in common with the holy war and crusade mentality, while Hubmaier's rationale for a defensive war was more in line with the just war approach. Even Menno Simons, from whom Mennonites get their name, hoped for pious magistrates who would use the sword to punish the wicked and protect the good. It is the small group of Swiss Anabaptists (Swiss Brethren) around Conrad Grebel, Felix Mantz, Georg Blaurock, and Michael Sattler who quickly developed into staunch separatists and pacifists. This is most dramatically reflected in the Schleitheim Articles of 1527, as we shall see below.

Separatist Pacifists

One could schematize the diverse attitudes of Anabaptists concerning the relationship between church and world and the use of the sword with four points on a spectrum. At one end of the spectrum are the Swiss Brethren, along with Peter Riedemann and the Hutterite Anabaptists, who rigorously set true believers over against the world and the state. Christians committed to live "inside the perfection of Christ" are not to participate in governments or use force. Governments, however, may use the "sword" (referring to the judicial and police-powers of the state) because God has given them the mandate to punish the wicked and protect the good "outside the perfection of Christ."

What has come to be known as the Schleitheim Confession consists of seven articles: on baptism, the ban, breaking of bread, separation from the world, the appointment of shepherds (pastors), use of the sword, and the swearing of oaths. Underlying the articles is a fundamental dualism between light and darkness, church and world: "Now there is nothing else in the world and all creation than good and evil, believing and unbelieving, darkness and light, the world and those who are [come] out of the world, God's temple and idols, Christ and Belial, and none will have part with the other."[1]

At the end of Article IV, on separation from the world, we read a clear prohibition against the use of weapons by Christians in the true church: "Thereby shall also fall away from us the diabolic weapons of violence—such as sword, armor, and the like, and all of their use to protect friends or against enemies—by virtue of the word of Christ: 'you shall not resist evil.'" This prohibition, however, does not apply to those in the world, as we find in Article VI:

> We have been united as follows concerning the sword. The sword is an ordering of God

outside the perfection of Christ. It punishes and kills the wicked, and guards and protects the good. In the law the sword is established over the wicked for punishment and for death, and secular rulers are established to wield the same. But within the perfection of Christ only the ban is used for the admonition and exclusion of the one who has sinned, without the death of the flesh, simply the warning and the command to sin no more.

This Article goes on to prohibit true Christians from participating in the government's task of punishing evil and protecting the good, and from being magistrates.

The Moravian Anabaptists, known as Hutterites, were close to the Swiss Anabaptists in their understanding of Christians and government. "The government is appointed by God as a rod of his anger, to discipline and punish evil and wicked people."[2] Christians are to be obedient to the authorities appointed by God to protect them, as far as conscience allows. However, the people of God "are not to use the worldly sword or rule with it. Instead, they should be led and ruled by the spirit of Christ." Governmental authority "was given in wrath, so it cannot find a place in Christ or be part of him. No Christian is a ruler, and no ruler is a Christian, for the child of blessing cannot be the servant of wrath. In Christ, temporal weapons are not used. Instead, spiritual weapons are used in such a way that people neither deserve nor need the methods of punishment or discipline used by the world."[3]

Thus Christians are forbidden to participate in any kind of war, in paying taxes that are meant for "war, executions, and bloodshed," and all making of swords, spears, muskets, or any kind of weapon. Nor are Christians allowed to judge and bring lawsuits against anyone.

Revolutionary Non-Pacifists

At the other end of the Anabaptist spectrum were the radical revolutionaries who considered themselves called to overthrow governments. These included early leaders such as Hubmaier who promoted the demands of the peasants, and Hans Hut who anticipated a time when the elect will unsheath their swords to assist in bringing in the kingdom. Thomas Müntzer was involved in the peasant revolt of 1525. The most dramatic example of revolutionary Anabaptism was the violent takeover of the city of Münster in 1534 by leaders who hoped to bring in God's Kingdom through a theocratic state.

Although Müntzer was technically not an Anabaptist (there is no evidence that he was rebaptized as an adult, the criterion for membership), he was a radical reformer who had followers, like Hut, who became leaders in the Anabaptist movement and influenced later Anabaptism. In his July 13, 1524, "Sermon to the Princes," one gets a good sense of Müntzer's theological and political views. The sermon is a diatribe against the clergy, a challenge to the princes, and a defense of the peasants. Clergy are accused of superstitious preaching, meaningless and even "devilish" ceremonies (including the Mass), and corrupt lifestyles.

Müntzer calls for the annihilation of the godless and the wicked, especially the clergy. Giving priority to revelations and visions that are accessible to the lower classes, he criticizes the learned ones who side with the clergy and the princes. The elect are the peasants who are inspired by the Holy Spirit. They have access to the Spirit through the inner Word, not "a wooden Christ." The method by which true visions can be distinguished from false visions is through suffering, the "abyss of the soul," the pain that comes through the interior way and detachment from the senses, which feed lusts of the flesh.

Müntzer urges the princes to use the office of the sword to punish the godless, and to destroy the followers of Luther (whom he calls "Brother Fattened-swine" and "Brother Soft-life"). Rulers are to come to the aid of the elect, primarily the peasants, in the great battle to transform the world. The empires of Babylon, the Persians, the Greeks, the Romans, and now the Holy Roman Empire, in which evil clergy and temporal lords "copulate" with each other, have come to an end. Reversing the usual interpretation of Romans 13, Müntzer uses it to rally the rulers and their subjects to overthrow the present social and political order and to inaugurate a new Christian society. Should the rulers not take up the challenge, the sword will be taken away from them and given to someone else, since the godless have no right to life.

Moderate Pacifists

At the center of the Anabaptist spectrum are those, like Menno Simons, who hope for pious rulers who might even join the church and could govern in a Christian way with a minimal use of force. This group allows a restrained participation of Christians in civil life and the social order. Pilgram Marpeck, a respected Anabaptist leader, was a civil servant all of his life but avoided, and even resigned from, positions in which he would have to enforce capital punishment. Menno is more "separatist" than Marpeck, but both allowed for a qualified Christian participation in government.

Menno is not totally consistent, sometimes eschewing all Christian use of the sword, as in his 1535 "The Blasphemy of John of Leiden," and sometimes assuming that magistrates can be appealed to on Christian grounds. The chief concern of Menno in the 1535 work above is to separate true believers—he has just been converted to the Anabaptist cause—from any connection to the disastrous behavior and idolatrous claims of the Münster Anabaptists who inaugurated a theocratic government in that city. "Christ did not want to be defended with Peter's sword," he writes. "How can a Christian then defend himself with it? . . . It is forbidden to us to fight with physical weapons." He recalls the fruits of the spirit—love, joy, peace, longsuffering, gentleness, goodness, faith, meekness, temperance—and reminds Christians that "not a word is said about taking up the carnal sword or repaying evil with evil."[4]

Menno is arguing against force to bring in the kingdom of God (as the Münsterites intended), or in matters of faith and conscience. The proper function of rulers and magistrates is to punish the wicked, not religious dissenters. In his *Foundation of Christian Doctrine*, Menno exhorts magistrates to be tolerant and to exercise their office in all reasonableness and true Christian piety:

> Therefore, dear sirs, take heed; this is the task to which you are called: namely, to chastise and punish, in the true fear of God with fairness and Christian discretion, manifest criminals, such as thieves, murderers. . . . Your task is to do justice between a man and his neighbor, to deliver the oppressed out of the hand of the oppressor; also to restrain by reasonable means, that is, without tyranny and bloodshed, manifest deceivers who so miserably lead poor helpless souls by hundreds of thousands into destruction.[5]

The civil sword is legitimate in the temporal sphere of wickedness but not in the church or kingdom of Christ where the spiritual sword (God's word) reigns.

Just-War Radicals

Finally, there are Anabaptists such as Balthasar Hubmaier who permit Christians to be engaged in a variety of government services and allow the use of the sword for self-defense, the maintenance of order and justice, and the protection of "all oppressed and subjugated people, widows, orphans, friends, and strangers without regard to persons according to the will and earnest command of God."[6]

Hubmaier's arguments bear further consideration. His 1527 work, "On the Sword," is a call for Christian government, in opposition to the views of Swiss Anabaptists and others who argue against all Christian participation in government and the use of the sword. Addressed to a Moravian nobleman, it was written only a few weeks before Hubmaier's imprisonment, which led to his execution as a heretic. In the article, he interprets fifteen biblical passages that he thinks have been erroneously understood by Anabaptists who reject the use of the sword. Citing a long list of antinomies in the Bible (like Isaiah's call to beat swords into plowshares, and the opposite call in Joel 3:10 to beat plows into swords), he argues that believers should not accept "half-truths and half-judgments" but look at the "whole truth."

In interpreting Christ's saying to Peter, "Put your sword back into the sheath," and "Whoever takes up the sword shall perish by the sword," Hubmaier uses a kind of just war argument: "Do you realize how Christ here confirms the sword, that one should punish those with it who practice by it their own violence and sacrilege. And those shall do that who are chosen for it, whoever they might be. Yet, it is certain that the more righteous they are the better and more orderly they will carry the sword according to God's will for the protection of the innocent and the fear of evildoers."[7]

Interpreting Christ's statement, "Who has put me as judge over you?" Hubmaier states:

> Realize that Christ does not here reject the office of the judge, because it is not to be rejected. . . . Rather, he points out that nobody should set himself up as a judge, unless he is called or chosen for it. That is why we have the election of burgomasters, village mayors and judges. Christ lets all of those stand to rule and judge with God and a good conscience over temporal and physical matters. However, he did not want to concern himself with them. He had not become human for that purpose; nor was he appointed to that end.[8]

Clearly separating the spiritual sphere from the temporal one, reminiscent of Luther's distinction between the two kingdoms, Hubmaier argues that God has given humanity two offices: the church, which uses the ban to discipline, and the government, which uses the sword, hopefully in a Christian manner.[9] In this way Hubmaier can justify capital punishment: "However, the government—I speak of just government—does not kill out of anger or move out of mockery and despising words, but by the order of God, which commands it earnestly to do away with the evil ones and hold the righteous in peace."[10]

It can be argued that the Anabaptist movement began with the revolutionaries involved in the peasant revolts who called for a radical new social and political order, and gradually evolved into a pacifist alternative community known as the "Free Church." After the first generation of Radical Reformers, it was the pacifist streams—Hutterites, Swiss Anabaptists, and North German-Dutch Mennonites—who survived the initial defeats and persecutions and continue to the present day as a witness to the nonviolent message of Christianity. Today, Mennonites are considered a Historic Peace Church, which later came to include the Society of Friends (Quakers) and the Church of the Brethren.

9

Enlightenment: Humanism and Peace

The Reformation era of the sixteenth century was followed by a century of devastating religious wars. The Thirty Years War in Europe (1618–1648) and the Puritan revolutionary wars in England and Ireland (1640s–1660s) are but two examples. These were Crusade-like conflicts driven by economic and political factors; religion played a decisive role as Catholics and Protestants fought each other for the control of territories.

Lisa Sowle Cahill explicitly links the Puritan Wars under Oliver Cromwell with the holy wars and Crusades of the past, showing how the very notions of nonviolent discipleship and following Jesus are now perverted in support of violence:

What unites Puritans and crusaders, and may in the end stand out as the central feature of a category that could comprehend both, is the elevation and cultivation of violence as a core meaning of faithful following of Christ. It can scarcely be denied that this is a perversion—not just a conflict-driven application—of the gospel as embodied in the life and teaching of Jesus and in his death on the cross. It is this fundamental sanctification which, especially in the case of the Crusades, is promoted through Bible-linked warfare imagery. Undergirded by the assurance that the fallen warrior will be granted an eternal reward, it encourages abandonment of compassion and moderation toward the enemy. Imitation of Christ can hardly function as a curb on violence once killing is assimilated into the very meaning of Christlike behavior.[1]

It was this gross distortion of the very notion of Christian love that caused a reaction against religion in general in the following era, often called the Enlightenment. Beginning in the eighteenth century, Enlightenment thinking has roots in the late Medieval and Humanist/Renaissance periods (for example, in the writings of Erasmus) and extends well into the nineteenth century. It was a reaction against precisely these kinds of religious wars and what critics saw as the inherent intolerance of religion and dogma.

This Enlightenment period has also been called the Age of Reason, characterized by a return to the "humanism" of classical Greek thought and values. The arguments against war were largely based on prudence and humanistic values, rather than on scripture or revelation. The Western world was by no means free of war in this Age of Reason, however, as illustrated by the French and American revolutions, the Anglo-American War of 1812 and the Civil War of the 1860s, the Franco-Prussian and Russo-Japanese wars, the Crimean and Boer wars, and the North American wars against aboriginal peoples, not to mention the slave trade and colonization.

Yet the Enlightenment brought with it a spirit of optimism, even utopianism, and hope that war could be overcome and peace could be established through reason, law, agreements, and international diplomacy. The nineteenth century, from the Congress of Vienna in 1815, which divided up Europe after the Napoleonic wars, to the beginning of World War I in 1914, has been known (somewhat misleadingly) as a century of comparative peace and major reform, including the anti-slavery movement, laws against child labor, prison improvements, women's suffrage, and temperance.

This optimism bore considerable fruit. In North America, numerous peace societies emerged among the Society of Friends

(Quakers), Unitarians, Methodists, Baptists, Congregationalists, and Presbyterians. There were also more radical pacifist groups, such as the Quakers' nonresistance society in England, and the Doukhobor and Tolstoyan communities in Russia. The Historic Peace Churches, like the Mennonite Church, continued their staunch pacifism through the American revolutionary and civil wars, basing their views not on optimistic notions about human perfectibility but on biblical revelation and the teachings of Jesus. The nineteenth century also saw a renewed emphasis on arbitration and disarmament, of which the Rush-Bagot Agreement of 1816, which established a demilitarized border between Canada and the United States, and the establishment of the Hague Tribunal in 1899 for adjudicating disputes are examples.

There are numerous thinkers that one could cite as examples of this age of law, tolerance, optimism, and hope for overcoming war between nations. Here we consider just two such thinkers and their works: Immanuel Kant and his *Perpetual Peace* (1795), and Leo Tolstoy and his works "Patriotism or Peace" (1896), "Patriotism and Government" (1900), and "Letter to Ernest Howard Crosby: On Non-Resistance" (1896).

Kant's Rationalism

Reason, according to Kant, guarantees perpetual peace. Its aim is to establish peace among human beings against their will and through their discord. While wars have separated people and driven them into far-flung areas of the world, people are still forced to live in lawful relations with each other. While by nature people are selfish and given to warring, by reason and law they are driven to peace. What is required, in Kant's view, are national and international state institutions to create and safeguard principles to ensure right and legal settlement of disputes.

True to his Enlightenment heritage, Kant has a progressive view of history, law, and the ultimate triumph of reason: "All politics," he says, "must bend its knee before the right. But by this it can hope slowly to reach the stage where it will shine with an immortal glory."[2] Perpetual peace will gradually, step by step, approach its ultimate goal. He envisions a world federation of states, something like a United Nations, an alliance based on principles of right. Perpetual peace is a moral and political ideal for Kant:

> Now our moral-practical reason pronounces its irresistible veto: There ought not to be war, neither that between me and thee in the state of nature nor that between us as states, which, though internally in a lawful condition, are

externally, in relation to each other, in a lawless condition. For war is not the way in which each one should seek his rights. . . . Rather, we must act as if that thing, perpetual peace, existed— though it may not exist; we must endeavour to make it real and strive after the constitution (perhaps the republicanism of each and every state) which seems to us most likely to bring it to pass and to make an end to the disastrous warmaking to which all states without exception have directed their institutions as their chief end. And if the achievement of this purpose were to remain always only a pious wish, certainly in assuming a maxim of incessantly striving toward it we would at least not delude ourselves, for this is duty.[3]

For Kant the best constitution is one based on sovereign law, realized through gradual reform based on the highest principles of right, perpetual peace, and the highest political good. We can see how idealistic are Kant's hopes for a peaceful world, based on law and Enlightenment assumptions of human reason and progress, assumptions that would be shattered by the wars of the twentieth century.

Tolstoy's Utopianism

Leo Tolstoy was more optimistic, even utopian, about the hope for peace and a world without war. He is well known, of course, for his epic novel *War and Peace*, but he wrote numerous other works on pacifism and the evils of nationalism. In one of these works, *The Kingdom of God Is within You*, Tolstoy provides a detailed history and defense of pacifism. The book is said to have been a major influence on Mohandas Gandhi.

In his 1896 letter, "Patriotism or Peace," Tolstoy argued that it is impossible to unite peace and patriotism. Seeking national power, wealth, and glory inevitably leads to war; in fact, all countries emerge from conquest and violence. Patriotism and war are both rooted in the exclusive desire for the good of one's own nation. "And so to abolish war, it is necessary to abolish patriotism, and to abolish patriotism, it is necessary first to become convinced that it is an evil, and that it is hard to do."[4] Patriotism is the legacy of barbarous times. It is incompatible not only with Christ's teachings but also with the morality of Christian society. As long as we extol patriotism we will ruin our countries through terrible wars.

In "Patriotism and Government," Tolstoy laments that all his arguments against patriotism have been met with silence. He repeats his conviction that the welfare of one's own nation is always at the expense of other nations, and thus patriotism stems the tide of progress.

Institutional religion, according to Tolstoy, propagates obsolete ideas such as patriotism in the minds of people, thus helping to retard the advance of civilization. Clerics and the ruling classes—politicians, capitalists, journalists, the majority of scholars and artists—maintain their advantageous positions in society by defending the patriotism at the heart of the political/social structures. Armies, money, schools, religion, and the press are all in the hands of these ruling classes. Even international bodies, like the Hague Tribunal, are unable to solve the problem of war because "as long as there shall exist governments with armies, the cessation of armaments and wars is impossible."[5]

Sounding like an anarchist, Tolstoy maintains that the notion of government, which he calls "that implement of violence . . . from which originate all the greatest calamities of men," has become not only unnecessary but dangerous to the world and should be abolished. Human beings, instead of recognizing themselves as children of God, as free beings guided by reason, see themselves as slaves of government, contrary to conscience and reason. Tolstoy is not a full-fledged anarchist—he is for the abolition of governments because they exercise violence but he is not for the destruction of all institutions. Those that are good and rational are to be supported: laws, courts, property, police, financial institutions, popular education. In other words, those institutions not dependent on violence are to be retained.

In his "Letter to Ernest Howard Crosby: On Non-Resistance," Tolstoy reveals the theological foundations of his views. Recognizing that one cannot force people to accept the principle of nonresistance, because that would contradict the principle itself, he explains the Christian stance: Nonresistance is not meant to become "a universal law for all humanity," as Kant proposed, "but what each man must do in order to fufill his destiny, to save his soul, and to do God's work."[6] Christian teaching does not prescribe laws for all people but addresses each person individually.

The rational meaning of life, for Tolstoy, consists in fulfilling God's will, not one's own. Here we see how closely he relates rationality with God's will. The Christian is called to contribute to the building of God's kingdom in this world. This entails acting amicably toward others—doing unto others what you would have them do unto you.

Tolstoy heaps scorn on those who call themselves Christians but depart from the law of God and the common good by participating in war and depriving others of liberty. As it is impossible for most people to "subject a child to torture and to kill it, though such a torture may save a hundred other people, so a whole series of acts becomes impossible for a man who has developed the Christian sensitiveness of his heart in himself."[7] Capital punishment, forcible seizure of someone else's property, declaration of war, or any act of violence are all impossible for one who lives a Christian life.

Tolstoy does recognize that violence may sometimes be inevitable, for example in restraining a criminal or protecting a child, but it can never be justified on Christian grounds. We may use violence under the pretext of the good; "but it is absolutely impossible to assert that, in doing so, we are professing Christ's teaching, because Christ arraigned that very deception."[8]

It can be argued that Kant and especially Tolstoy were unrealistic idealists when it came to the question of abolishing war between people and states. Nevertheless, they represent a strong abhorrence of the religiously legitimated wars of the previous era. Kant is the rationalist for whom war is irrational. Tolstoy is the utopian who holds patriotism largely responsible for all wars and who condemns the notion that one can ever kill in the name of Jesus Christ.

Although neither Kant nor Tolstoy professes to represent the institutional church, they reflect the spirit of humanism, rationalism, and optimism that was present in the liberalism of nineteenth-century Christianity, manifested especially in the missionary movement.

10

Twentieth Century I: Age of Realism

The eighteenth and nineteenth centuries were by no means free of wars and various forms of violence, as we have seen in the previous chapter. Nevertheless, the nineteenth century was an age of comparative peace in the West. This century of optimism and confidence in human progress came to an end in 1914, with the beginning of World War I. By the end of this war, in 1918, the Western world had lost any naive illusions about progress and the possibility of peace.

World War I: Holy War

This was a new type of war, a total war, with the nations divided into two opposing camps: the Allies (including England, France, Canada, the United States) and the Central Powers (Germany, Austria, Hungary, Italy). Although some paid lip service to just war principles, claiming God and justice were on their side, the rhetoric took on the character of a holy war, particularly in England and the United States.

In the words of Roland Bainton, "In the United States the mood was a blend of hysterical nationalism and crusading idealism.[1] This was hailed as a war to end all wars, a battle to "make the world safe for democracy." Bainton claims that "American churchmen of all faiths were never so united with each other and with the mind of the country. This was a holy war, Jesus was dressed in khaki and portrayed sighting down a gun barrel. The Germans were Huns."[2]

On the German side, there was a similar holy war fusion of crown and altar, with the vast majority of men signing up enthusiastically to fight for God and Fatherland, fed by Romantic notions of racial and national superiority. In Germany, Mennonites had largely shed their pacifist heritage and signed up to fight along with their countrymen.

Voices opposing the war were in the minority. In England, outspoken pacifists included such luminaries as writer Aldous Huxley and philosopher Bertrand Russell, who was imprisoned for his anti-war activities. In the United States, according to Bainton, there were only eighty pacifist clergymen, but this number obviously does not include the many pacifist pastors and members of the Historic Peace Churches who refused to go to war. Besides the many conscientious objectors who served in non-combatant roles, about two thousand American pacifists during World War I were imprisoned because of their absolute refusal to cooperate with the military in any way. Many were violently mistreated, leading to the deaths of two Hutterite prisoners (Gingerich). Another example of anti-war sentiment was the establishment in December 1914 of the Fellowship of Reconciliation, founded by Presbyterian minister Richard Roberts and Quaker Henry Hodgkin.

Canadian Mennonites and Amish, who were exempt from military service by law, managed to keep that exemption intact when conscription was mandated in 1917, but their position was not without much confusion and conflict with authorities and the public during the war.

Interwar Years: Pacifism

The war ended with Germany's capitulation and the humiliating terms of the Versailles Treaty, including the infamous clause demanding that Germany accept sole guilt for the war. The resulting bitterness and deprivation suffered by the Germans because of severe reparation demands sowed the seeds for the rise of National Socialism and World War II. In Germany, the war was followed by an experiment in democracy, the Weimar Republic, which lasted from 1919 until Adolph Hitler's grasp of totalitarian power in 1933. In the United States, the crusading spirit of the war was replaced by the "crusade for an enduring peace."

Many ecclesiastical leaders, such as Harry Emerson Fosdick, became pacifists. American churches embarked on a mission for peace, looking to the state to eliminate war, to the church to excommunicate war, and to the community to find alternatives to war. Most churches, however, other than the Historic Peace Churches (Mennonites, Quakers, Church of the Brethren), were not ready to commit themselves to absolute pacifism, although they supported treaties calling for the "renunciation of war as an instrument of national policy."[3] The World Court and the League of Nations were hailed as alternatives to war and received hearty support from many churches.

Despite this post-war optimism and crusade for peace, new theological movements were assaulting liberal notions of humanity and progress. Karl Barth and Reinhold Niebuhr were two such voices, emphasizing human sinfulness and the impossibility of eliminating war and conflict, although Barth was a virtual pacifist. Niebuhr was respectful of the biblical nonresistance of peace churches, such as the Mennonites, but he had nothing but scorn for liberal views that assumed pacifism could be adopted as a political strategy. This was confirmed for Niebuhr by the rise of Hitler and totalitarianism.

World War II: Realism

During World War II, Americans moved gradually from isolationism to involvement in world affairs, belatedly entering the war against the Nazis. Most churches reluctantly gave up their convictions never to support another war. In the words of Bainton, "To be sure, the war might not establish democracy, liberty, and a just and enduring peace. The only thing the war can ever do is to restrain outrageous villainy and give a chance to build again. A victory of the Allies would ensure none of the ideal ends which Christians entertained, but a victory for the Axis would preclude them. And an Axis victory could be prevented only by military strength."[4]

This was not a holy war, and it did not have unanimous church support. In the United States, three thousand ministers joined the Quaker-sponsored Fellowship of Reconciliation as a sign of their pacifist convictions. About twelve thousand American draftees chose Civilian Public Service instead of joining the military. At the same time, many former pacifists, especially after the Japanese attack on Pearl Harbor, gave up their pacifism and joined the ranks of the war supporters. Among Canadian Mennonites, just over 7,500 chose alternative service, while 4,500 enlisted in the military.[5]

The *Christian Century* proposed a fourth position beyond pacifism, crusade, and just war: this was "just war," not a just war. The irony of this new term, one which did not glorify war or justify it, was that the war against Germany became even more ruthless than the ones before. War became "degraded," with the goal of winning by whatever means, even obliteration bombing to demoralize a noncombatant population. The German blanket bombing of London, the Allied fire bombing of Dresden, and the American atomic bombing of Nagasaki and Hiroshima are but four examples. As Winston Churchill said in 1943: "There are no sacrifices we will not make, no lengths of violence to which we will not go."[6]

Niebuhr and Christian Realism

Reinhold Niebuhr, the greatest American ethicist of the twentieth century, gave up his pacifism after World War I. He had earlier been chair of the Fellowship of Reconciliation. In the introduction to his 1940 collection of essays, *Christianity and Power Politics*, Niebuhr repudiates modern secular and Christian perfectionism that does not allow for participation in conflict, calling it a "very sentimentalized version of the Christian faith" that is at variance with the deepest insights of Christianity.[7] Liberal perfectionism does not distinguish between tyranny and freedom. "It does not realize that its effort to make the peace of the Kingdom of God into a simple historical possibility must inevitably result in placing a premium upon surrender to evil."[8] This form of perfectionism, says Niebuhr, is both bad religion and bad politics.

In the first essay of the volume, "Why the Christian Church Is Not Pacifist," Niebuhr argues that the failure of the church to espouse pacifism is not apostasy, as some claim, but grows out of the gospel itself. The good news of the gospel is not the law of love but that there is a "divine mercy which is able to overcome a contradiction within our own souls, which we cannot ourselves overcome."[9]

Sin is a persistent factor in human history and society. Most modern forms of pacifism are heretical in their denial of the sinfulness and tragedy of human existence, with the following exceptions: the perfectionism of medieval asceticism and the sectarian perfectionism of a Menno Simons (Mennonites). In these cases, the law of love is not proposed as a political alternative but the political task itself is disavowed. In fact, according to Niebuhr, the Mennonites are a legitimate reminder to other Christians that the norms of social justice are not absolute.

Niebuhr argues that Jesus' injunctions to "resist not evil" and to "love your enemies" are absolute and uncompromising. They are absolute norms, but human beings can never attain them. He has no use for just war proponents who try to justify their actions by domesticating the teachings and example of Jesus. What Jesus espouses is not nonviolent resistance but nonresistance. This leaves us with the paradox of belief in the high moral demands of Jesus and the human inability to act accordingly.

The reason for this paradox is the contradiction between the law of love and the sinfulness of humanity. "It is because men are sinners that justice can be achieved only by a certain degree of coercion on the one hand, and by resistance to coercion and tyranny on the other hand. The political life of man must constantly steer between the Scylla of anarchy and the Charybdis of tyranny."[10] Refusal to recognize sin is to give in to the preference of tyranny over war. The kingdom of God is no simple historical possibility. And yet, the law of love remains the principle by which to judge all forms of community, of coercion, and of justice. Niebuhr's main concern is the prevention of anarchy, on the one side, and tyranny, on the other. Democratic societies have the best chance of preventing both.

John Howard Yoder's Critique

Niebuhr's nemesis is John Howard Yoder, who views Niebuhr as the most important challenge to the pacifist position. Yoder's booklet, *Reinhold Niebuhr and Christian Pacifism*, points out the agreements and disagreements between them. The points of agreement are the following: the New Testament teaches nonresistance, not nonviolent resistance (although Yoder seems to soften his position in *The Politics of Jesus*); the ultimate ethical norm for ethics is love; compromise endangers good ends; both sides are selfish in war, politics, and police action, and religious interest ought not to be identified with war; some pacifists (especially the liberal kind of the interwar years) are overly optimistic; nonviolence and nonresistance are to be distinguished—the Gandhian type of pacifism is really a form of nonviolent coercion, not nonresistance; and one cannot expect a Christian degree of unselfishness and love in society in general.

There are, however, major differences. Niebuhr, says Yoder, depreciates the horrors of war and makes no serious differentiation between war and policing. Nor does he distinguish between being an active moral agent in violence and the refusal to use violence in the face of evil. For example, Yoder would not agree that enduring slavery is worse than waging war against it. In his use of terms like "impossibility" (of following the Jesus ethic), "necessity" (of doing the lesser evil), and "responsibility" (for the world), Niebuhr introduces new norms into ethics which because of sin are allowed to cancel out the normativity of love.

Niebuhr believes that the fact of sin relativizes moral action and what can be done in given situations. Yoder, who agrees that sin is a fact in the world, rejects Niebuhr's notion that you can derive moral and ethical principles from this fact. For Yoder, an "ought" can never be derived from an "is." Niebuhr considers a selfish motive such as self-preservation as an ethical determinant and can thereby justify compromises that his own country makes in its foreign policy. His ethical pluralism, says Yoder, allows for contradictory positions to coexist with each other. It assumes that the divine will cannot be known and acted upon in given situations.

However, Yoder raises more profound objections against Niebuhr. He undervalues the biblical view of resurrection as enabling grace, not merely as forgiving and justifying grace. There is in Niebuhr a virtual absence of any doctrine of the church. In the Bible, the bearer of the meaning of history is not one's country but a divine-human society (the church). According to Yoder, the church is the one example where the group is more moral than the individual, contradicting Niebuhr's thesis in his *Moral Man and Immoral Society*, where he claims that the group is always more immoral than the individual.

Furthermore, Niebuhr does not distinguish between believer and nonbeliever. There is no place in his theological ethics for the doctrine of conversion and regeneration. The real problem is that he illegitimately unites Christian and non-Christian elements in his social-ethical theory. Niebuhr neglects the doctrine of the Holy Spirit as the power within history and especially within the church that enables one to act according to the love taught by Christ. According to Yoder, sin is vanquished every time the Christian in the power of the Holy Spirit chooses obedience to the Spirit instead of political or national necessity.

11

Twentieth Century II:
Nuclear Pacifism

World War II ended with the obliteration fire bombing of German cities like Dresden and Hamburg, and finally with the first use of atomic weapons, dropped by the Americans on the cities of Nagasaki and Hiroshima. This event ushered in the atomic age and the Cold War. The use of nuclear weapons raised entirely new questions for Christian moralists on war and Christian participation in war. While there were some, like Reinhold Niebuhr, who left open the possibility of using nuclear weapons in extreme cases, or at least threatening to use them as a deterrent, by the mid-1980s there was wide agreement among mainstream Christian denominations and Historic Peace Churches that no nuclear war could possibly meet the requirements of just war criteria. Nuclear war must therefore be denounced, along with the buildup of nuclear stockpiles for deterrence and potential use.

Canadian Churches Protest

Canadian churches were on the forefront in passing resolutions against nuclear weapons and urging the government, on theological and political grounds, to intervene in the growing nuclear crisis. Churches also spread their message through Project Ploughshares, a highly respected research and lobby organization founded in 1976 to monitor arms sales. Ploughshares was sponsored by the Canadian Council of Churches and supported by a wide range of churches, development agencies, and individuals. Its studies and publications made a strong case for nuclear disarmament and the immorality of all nuclear war.

In a 1984 paper on "The Church and Nuclear Disarmament," Project Ploughshares published two briefs of Canadian churches to Prime Minister Pierre Trudeau, who had just undertaken some courageous international peace initiatives. The paper also included church statements on nuclear disarmament by the Anglican Church, United Church of Canada, Conference of Catholic Bishops, Lutheran and Presbyterian churches, Mennonites, and Society of Friends.

These church statements are clear and unanimous: "We must say without reservation that nuclear weapons are ultimately unacceptable as agents of national security. We can conceive of no circumstances under which the use of nuclear weapons could be justified and consistent with the will of God, and we must therefore conclude that nuclear weapons must also be rejected as means of threat or deterrence." The churches ground their expressions theologically:

> Above all, our attention to questions of war and peace is informed by the reconciliation that is promised us in the ministry, death and resurrection of Jesus Christ. In Him there is no East or West, no North or South—under His reign all are one. We do not, therefore, accept the division of the world into allies and enemies—and those who have been defined as our enemies, we regard as brothers and sisters whose welfare must remain our paramount concern.[1]

We might call this growing consensus among churches a "nuclear pacifism," distinguished from the traditional pacifism of the peace churches in that it does not condemn all warfare and maintains the right of sovereign states to protect their territories by conventional means. Behind this unanimity is the conviction that nuclear war is different from other war. "The moral principle, of course, is the acknowledgement that nuclear weapons are of a fundamentally different character than other weapons and that the legitimate rights of states to arrange for their national defense do not include the right to initiate nuclear war."[2]

The Canadian Catholic bishops go further to identify the economic injustice that lies at the root of conflict:

> We do maintain that nations have a right to engage in just struggles to defend their national sovereignty. Similarly, repressed peoples have the right to struggle for the overthrow of tyrants when all democratic means are frustrated. . . . The roots of . . . injustice are found in the very structures of the world's economic order. For the present economic order perpetuates a systematic cycle of poverty, dependency, and repression. . . . While these countries have the right to defend their population against aggression, our concern has to do with the vast amounts of money that are spent on military arms rather than serving the basic social and economic needs of people in those countries and Canada's role in perpetuating this problem.[3]

Similarly, the United Church of Canada roots the problem of war and arms buildup in the context of larger inequities:

> Disarmament and its shadow-side, militarization, are symptoms of a fundamental

insecurity that threatens the survival of all people. Other symptoms threatening people are related to the military threat: poverty, hunger, oppression, environmental deterioration, depletion of natural resources, population explosions, and so on. Therefore, disarmament and militarization cannot be left to the people who analyze military strategy or plan defense budgets. Nor can it be treated as just one problem among many.[4]

Mennonites, as could be expected of a peace church, come up with an unequivocal rejection of all military participation: "War is contrary to the will of God. Activities and attitudes which contribute to war are sinful . . . we believe that followers of our Lord cannot in good conscience serve in the military forces or request military protection from their governments."[5] The Society of Friends (Quakers) assert:

Because the concept of 'the nation' is one of the main justifications for the claim for security through armaments, as Friends we have to free ourselves from the fear that the supreme institution 'nation' may be attacked by other 'nations' for whatever cause. Our loyalty is to humanity above all nations. We must see ourselves as citizens of the Kingdom of God.[6]

American Catholic Bishops

The protest against increased militarization and nuclear deterrence went well beyond any one country. In a 1983 pastoral letter on war and peace, "The Challenge of Peace: God's Promise and Our Response," the National [American] Conference of Catholic Bishops came out with a ringing rejection of nuclear weapons: "Under no circumstances may nuclear weapons or other instruments of mass slaughter be used for the purpose of destroying population centers or other predominantly civilian targets." The letter continues, "We do not perceive any situation in which the deliberate initiation of nuclear war, on however restricted a scale, can be morally justified. Non-nuclear attacks by another state must be resisted by other than nuclear means."[7]

The bishops go still further, however. While not rejecting unequivocally the concept of deterrence, they declare "support [for] immediate, bilateral verifiable agreements to halt the testing, production and deployment of new nuclear weapon systems." Together with the Pope, they call for a "moral about face" in which the world says "no to nuclear conflict; no to weapons of mass destruction; no to an arms race which robs the poor and the vulnerable; and no to the moral danger of a nuclear age."[8]

Although the bishops begin the document by saying, "Catholic teaching in every case begins with a presumption against war,"[9] the bishops fall short of condemning all warfare. This stance has been roundly criticized by theologians such as Stanley Hauerwas. Hauerwas argues that in both Pope John XXIII's *Pacem in Terris* and the American Catholic Bishops' letter, there is a theologically untenable paradox that is due to an inadequate ecclesiology and eschatology, one which postpones radical obedience to Jesus' teaching of nonviolence by the church as whole to some future time.[10]

Nevertheless, in what is a new emphasis, the Catholic bishops come out endorsing "peacemaking" and even pacifism as a legitimate, church-supported Catholic option based on the New Testament teaching of Jesus Christ: "Peace-making is not an optional commitment. It is a requirement of our faith. We are called to be peacemakers, not by some movement of the moment, but by our Lord Jesus Christ. The content and context of our peacemaking is set not by some political agenda or ideological program, but by the teaching of the Church."

In the end, however, the Pastoral Letter continues to hold to the traditional complex moral position of the Catholic Church, including the just war tradition based on reason and natural law, distinguishing between the "community of the faithful" and the "civil community." The letter says:

> The religious community shares a specific perspective of faith and can be called to live out its implications. The civil community, although it does not share the same vision of faith, is equally bound by certain key moral principles. For all men and women find in the depth of their consciences a law written on the human heart by God. From this law reason draws moral norms. These norms do not exhaust the gospel vision, but they speak to critical questions affecting the welfare of the human community, the role of states in international relations, and the limits of acceptable action by individuals and nations on issues of war and peace.[11]

The bishops then go into a rather detailed explication and defense of just war criteria. "Just-war teaching has evolved, however, as an effort to prevent war; only if war cannot be rationally avoided, does the teaching then seek to restrict and reduce its horrors. It does this by establishing a set of rigorous conditions which must be met if the decision to go to war is to be morally permissible. Such a decision, especially today, requires extraordinarily strong reasons for overriding the presumption *in favor of peace* and *against* war."[12]

Citing the examples of pacifists such as Francis of Assisi, Mahatma Gandhi, Dorothy Day, and Martin Luther King Jr., along with the *Pastoral Constitution* of Vatican II, the bishops explicitly defend those Christians who reject all war in the light of Jesus' teachings and adopt a position of conscientious objection to participation in the military. They recognize the "development of a theology of peace and the growth of the Christian pacifist position among Catholics." The letter states: "While the just-war teaching has clearly been in possession for the past 1,500 years of Catholic thought, the 'new movement' in which we find ourselves sees the just-war teaching and non-violence as distinct but interdependent methods of evaluating warfare. They diverge on some specific conclusions, but they share a common presumption against the use of force as a means of settling disputes."[13]

The following statement more than any other reflects the paradoxical, perhaps contradictory, position of the American Catholic bishops.

> We believe work to develop non-violent means of fending off aggression and resolving conflict best reflects the call of Jesus both

to love and to justice. Indeed, each increase in the potential destructiveness of weapons and therefore of war serves to underline the rightness of the way that Jesus mandated to his followers. But, on the other hand, the fact of aggression, oppression and injustice in our world also serves to legitimate the resort to weapons and armed force in defense of justice. We must recognize the reality of the paradox we face as Christians living in the context of the world as it presently exists, we must continue to articulate our belief that love is possible and the only real hope for all human relations, and yet accept that force, even deadly force, is sometimes justified and that nations must provide for their defense. It is the mandate of Christians, in the face of this paradox, to strive to resolve it through an even greater commitment to Christ and his message.[14]

In this chapter, we have seen how the threat of nuclear war has brought churches into closer unity than ever before on the issues of war and peace. Despite the somewhat equivocal tone of the Catholic bishops' letter, for example, there is still an underlying movement toward a more explicit peace witness based on the person and teachings of Jesus Christ.

12

Postmodernity:
Terror and the War on Terror

Many say that on September 11, 2001, the world changed forever as a group of religiously motivated terrorists flew planes into the World Trade Center towers in New York City and the Pentagon in Washington, D.C. Estimates are that 3,119 persons were killed, 2,895 of them in New York City. On that morning, I was driving to Toronto to teach my first class of the term. I heard on my car radio that a plane had hit the World Trade Center. When I arrived at the Toronto School of Theology, I watched in astonishment as the twin towers collapsed. At 11:00 a.m. I began teaching my class on "War and Peace in Christian Thought." Teacher and students were electrified by the dramatic events and how graphically they illustrated the topic of the course.

During those first days and weeks after the attack, there was an outpouring of sympathy

for American citizens from countries and people
all over the world: Muslims, Jews, Hindus, Sikhs,
Buddhists, Christians, and many others. All were
anxiously waiting to see how the United States
would respond, and asking searching questions
about the meaning of the attacks. Why does
God allow such evil and violence? What should
be the Christian response?

Voices against a War on Terror

In the wake of the attacks, a Mennonite
press quickly published a book, *Where Was
God on Sept. 11? Seeds of Faith and Hope*.
It was a collection of essays, sermons, inter-
views, and letters echoing the thoughts and
feelings of more than seventy religious leaders and thinkers struggling with the question of faith in God in the midst of terror.
While the authors represent different points
of view, there is a united condemnation of
violence of all kinds, including vengeance,
and a call for nonviolent alternatives to deal
with terror.

The Mennonite Central Committee, in a
September 22 statement, represented the Historic Peace Church tradition in a call for love
of enemy and a refusal to participate in violence: "Throughout its history, MCC has stood
against a culture of violence by witnessing

against war preparation, enemy demoniza-
tion, and the use of military force to solve
difficult international problems."[1]

In Canada, a coalition of ecumenical organizations, including the Canadian Council
of Churches, Kairos: Canadian Ecumenical
Justice Initiatives, and Project Ploughshares,
made continuing appeals to the Canadian government to move with caution in responding
to the terrorist attacks and to reject the option
of war against Afghanistan and, later, Iraq.

In a September 25, 2002, letter to Prime
Minister Jean Chretien, a broad spectrum of
Canadian church leaders wrote:

> We write, as leaders in many Christian com-
> munities in Canada, to cry NO to such a war.
> This is a time for intense diplomacy and
> face-to-face negotiations, not for missiles
> and high-altitude bombing. This is especially
> a time for multilateralism. . . . Yes, the world
> is faced with a dangerous situation, in Iraq
> and in the Middle East region as a whole.
> But non-military, peace-building approaches
> to those grave problems are thinkable and
> possible—and they are infinitely preferable
> to war.[2]

In a detailed presentation on Iraq to the
House of Commons Standing Committee on

Foreign Affairs and International Trade on
November 18, 2002, Ernie Regehr, director of
Project Ploughshares, said:

> To understand where the march toward war in
> Iraq can finally be expected to lead we need
> but recall the story of the twentieth century.
> Unprecedented in both numbers and destruc-
> tiveness, the wars of the century just ended
> were fought to restore peace, democracy, and
> human rights, and, indeed, to end all war, but
> their accumulated legacy is of unprecedented
> numbers of lives lost, of resources wasted,
> and of an international order still short on
> peace, democracy, and human rights, and still
> poised for, and extensively engaged in, ever
> more war. It is the reality that led the found-
> ers of the United Nations to declare its cen-
> tral aim to be 'to save succeeding generations
> from the scourge of war.' The international
> community will not reach maturity and sta-
> bility, and people in states like Iraq will not
> enjoy safety and well being, as long as we
> collectively hold to the discredited view that
> war is the means to its opposite. War sows
> more war—the twentieth century confirms
> that as a general truth and it is our responsi-
> bility to recognize that unavoidable truth in
> specific situations, like the Iraq of the early
> twenty-first century."[3]

A January 2003 joint statement by the Canadian Council of Churches, Kairos, and Project Ploughshares, "Prepare for Peace in Iraq," was sent out to parishes and congregations across Canada. It agrees that there should be a way of verifying that Iraq has rejected weapons of mass destruction but argues that "neither war nor the status quo is a means of assuring that important objective." It offers a series of positive, realistic, and transformative approaches to Iraq. Over the following weeks the statement was endorsed by more than forty thousand individuals and 370 churches from most Christian denominations across Canada. The results were forwarded to Prime Minister Chretien and may have influenced his decision that Canada would not support the United States in a war against Iraq, although it would agree to send troops to Afghanistan.

In Europe and the United States, there was also strong opposition to war against Iraq. In a World Council of Churches press release of February 3, 2003, three American church leaders joined twenty-two church leaders in Europe and the Middle East in calling for a peaceful resolution of the conflict. As reported by Project Ploughshares, "The leaders deplored the fact that the United States and other nations 'regard war as an acceptable instrument of foreign policy' and rejected the aims of the United States to use a 'pre-emptive military strike' to remove the Iraqi regime. They also called on the government of Iraq to comply with United Nations demands that it destroy all weapons of mass destruction."[4] The American leaders who added their names to the statement were the general secretaries of the National Council of Churches of Christ in the U.S.A., the General Board of Church and Society of the United Methodist Church, U.S.A., and the Division for Church and Society of the Evangelical Lutheran Church in America, U.S.A.

After war against Iraq was declared in March 2003 by American President George W. Bush, the Canadian Council for International Co-operation, representing a number of nongovernmental organizations, congratulated the Canadian Prime Minister for refusing to join in what they called the "illegal war." Ernie Regehr of Project Ploughshares disputed the U.S. Secretary of State Colin Powell's claim that the war was authorized by United Nations Resolution 1441 and "supported by international law." Regehr said: "Resolution 1441 in no way approves military action. In light of the catastrophic cost of war and the humanitarian disaster that will follow, it is immoral for the U.S. to bomb Iraq under the cloak of the United Nations."[5]

On March 20, 2003, the General Secretary of the World Council of Churches condemned the pre-emptive war against Iraq as "immoral, illegal and ill-advised." He said further:

> With profound sorrow I recognize that the United States, the United Kingdom and Spain, three members of the United Nations (UN) Security Council, have gone to war ignoring the voice of civil society, of the churches and of other faith communities in those countries and worldwide. I condemn this rush to unilateral military attack. Nonviolent means to solve the conflict have been far from exhausted. Disarmament of Iraq could have been achieved without a war. . . .
>
> The implicit unilateralism, by the U.S., the U.K. and Spain, contradict the spirit, ideal and prospect of multilateralism, the fundamental principles laid out in the UN Charter, and may damage hopes to create a strong international order in the post-Cold War period. . . . The response from churches against the war in Iraq has been an unprecedented manifestation of unanimity. The energy that has been released bears witness to a spirituality that calls for peaceful coexistence of all nations and peoples in accordance with the principles

enshrined in the UN Charter. That energy must not be lost. Churches should continue their united efforts to stop the war, to give assistance to those in need and to cooperate with people of other faiths, especially Muslims, to restore confidence and trust among the nations of the world.[6]

While massive protests against war in Iraq, and also Afghanistan, took place throughout the world, including the United States, there were also those who strongly defended the American right to wage war against terror and to defend militarily American values and way of life against those who would seek to destroy them.

Voices for a Just War against Terror

Is the just war still relevant in a world of terrorism? Oliver O'Donovan of the University of Edinburgh is one of the most respected defenders of the just war tradition, from Augustine to Aquinas to "classical" just war theory in the early modern period, to the present. Formerly professor of moral and pastoral theology at Christ Church, Oxford, O'Donovan was a student of American just war ethicist Paul Ramsey. In his 2003 volume, *The Just War Revisited*, written after September 11 but before the Iraq War, O'Donovan rethinks traditional just war principles and adapts them to the contemporary situation, including counter-insurgency and terrorist movements.

He argues that during the *saeculum* (the historical age between the time of Christ and the future kingdom of God) the church needs to engage in practical reasoning and make moral-philosophical judgments, including when society ought to take up arms. Unlike absolute pacifists, the church cannot avoid the question of moral and ethical judgments about declaring and conducting war.

A passionate supporter for a just war against terrorists and countries that harbor them is Jean Bethke Elshtain, ethicist from the University of Chicago. In her powerful book, *Just War against Terror*, she criticizes pacifists and others who reject military solutions to the crisis, and intellectuals who look for the root causes of terrorism as an alternative to military response. Agreeing with Michael Walzer, a Jewish American political philosopher, Elshtain distinguishes between terrorism (the term *terror* coming into our vocabulary with the French Revolution), and legitimate forms of killing. Not only do terrorists fail to distinguish between combatants and noncombatants, they deliberately and randomly target innocent people in order to instill fear in a general population.[7]

Unlike the just war tradition, which recognizes stringent limits to military engagement, terrorists are indiscriminate. They "hate us for *what we are and what we represent and not for anything in particular we have done.*"[8] She supports George Bush's declaration of war against terror on September 20, 2001, based on just principles, not revenge. Bush distinguished between Islam as a great religion and terrorists bent on hijacking their own religion in their hatred of American values. The fight against terror is fought against "all who believe in progress and pluralism, tolerance and freedom."[9]

Firmly Augustinian and Niebuhrian in her views, Elshtain says that resort to force may be a form of obedience to the Christian ethic of loving the neighbor. She acknowledges that all war is tragic and ambiguous, yet it is sometimes necessary for the sake of justice in a sinful world. Here is how she puts it:

> Absolute pacifists hold that the use of force is never justified under any circumstances. This form of pacifism is associated with the practices of early Christians who tied

their pacifism to certain ascetical norms and withdrawal from the world. Leaders charged with right authority within organized political bodies cannot withdraw from the world, of course, and thus are never pacifists. Anyone who accepts political leadership understands that he or she may be compelled to sanction the resort to force in certain circumstances. The just war tradition limits those circumstances in part because it shares with pacifism a strong presumption against violence and force, all other things being equal. The just war tradition does not discourage acts of forgiveness and reconciliation in political life but does recognize their limits in a world of conflicting human wills, one in which the ruthless would prevail if they faced neither restraint nor the prospect of punishment.[10]

The war against terror is a just cause, Elshtain argues. Terrorism is "an act of aggression aimed specifically at killing civilians," and just war is a way of exercising justice against acts of terror that aim at disrupting "fundamental civic peace and tranquility."[11] Elshtain was principal author of a February 2002 manifesto, "What We Are Fighting For," signed by sixty academics and intellectuals from diverse religious and secular backgrounds. The manifesto evokes the just war tradition in the fight against terror: both in the reasons for fighting and the means of fighting (that is, always keeping in mind the norms of justice and restraint, especially proportionality and discrimination).

The document highlights the fundamental values of the American way of life that are being threatened by terrorists of the September 11 attack, and contends that these are legitimate cause for war:

> 1. All human beings are born free and equal in dignity and rights. 2. The basic subject of society is the human person, and the legitimate role of government is to protect and help to foster the conditions for human flourishing. 3. Human beings naturally desire to seek the truth about life's purpose and ultimate ends. 4. Freedom of conscience and religious freedom are inviolable rights of the human person. 5. Killing in the name of God is contrary to faith in God and is the greatest betrayal of the universality of religious faith.[12]

The signatories believe these values to be universal, applicable to all peoples and all religions, and consistent with the 1940s United Nations Universal Declaration of Human Rights. They conclude with the following ringing endorsement: "Organized killers with global reach now threaten all of us. In the name of universal human morality, and fully conscious of the restrictions and requirements of a just war, we support our government's, and our society's, decisions to use force of arms against them."[13]

Conclusion

We have seen how the wars in Iraq and Afghanistan have once again divided the international community, although it is remarkable how strong and unified the anti-war voices have been within the religious community. Some in the international community have argued that terrorism is a new form of violence and requires a new form of response. Although we can't say that terrorism is a new phenomenon in history, there is something about contemporary terrorism the world over that is distinctive, reflecting the fragmented perceptions of reality and new forms of tribalism that are part of our post-modern era.

Pre-modern and modern forms of the just war were premised on universal rules of reason that have come under fire in postmodernity. Today's terrorism does not abide by any rules of war; and some have argued, in response, that the war against terrorism also need not abide by the normal rules of war, never mind just war. But as we have seen above, even those theorists who support a war against terror hold to some form of just war principles. There is still much thinking to be done. In the next chapter we will look at an alternative to military force in dealing with violence in the contemporary world.

13

Policing, Human Security, and the Responsibility to Protect

In this book, I have tried to portray as fairly as possible the various Christian approaches to the issue of war and peace throughout history. I have done so without hiding my own pacifist heritage and leanings. In this chapter, and the subsequent conclusion, I become more constructive in my approach, offering the reader my own theological-ethical defense and justification for "policing" as an alternative to war. This chapter explores how Christians might understand and rationalize participation in policing without compromising their underlying commitment to Jesus' way of peace, nonviolence, and reconciliation.[1]

The church as church cannot theologically justify the active taking of human life in any circumstance, including that of war or policing. And yet, might lethal force not sometimes be necessary to protect vulnerable people? This is the dilemma for Christians. To what extent individual Christians can participate in the mandate of the state to police, which may sometimes require lethal force, will depend, I argue, on the individual conscience guided by the discretion of a discerning community.

Policing under the just rule of law, whose aim is to restrain evil and maintain order for the common good, can certainly be distinguished from the military and its culture of killing.[2] In what follows, we will look at the recent international concern for human security and the responsibility to protect vulnerable populations, which might be characterized as "policing" or "peacekeeping" rather than "war-making." We will also look at traditional pacifist teaching on the subject and conclude with a look at "just policing" as an approach that both pacifists and traditional just war traditions might agree upon.

Human Security and the Responsibility to Protect

In the past few decades, the international church and political communities have struggled with their responsibility to protect people who find themselves in extraordinary situations of violence and violation of human rights, sometimes by their own governments. Rwanda is a dramatic example. The Commission of the Churches on International Affairs, a commission of the World Council of Churches, a few years ago brought together representatives from diverse national, theological, and political traditions to address the responsibility to protect and the potential need for force in such situations.

Ernie Regehr represented Project Ploughshares, the church-based research institute on the arms trade, at the WCC consultation and reported on the event. There appears to be growing support for the responsibility to protect as an international norm. While national governments have the primary responsibility to provide safety for their people, when they fail to do so the international community has the duty to intervene in the government's internal affairs.

Broad agreement exists among churches that the best way of protecting people in places like Darfur, the Republic of Congo, Northern Uganda, Rwanda, Cambodia, and Southern Sudan is to help provide basic needs and rights, assure social and political integration, and bring about de-escalation of political and criminal violence. This may call for coercive force. According to Regehr:

> Churches are not prepared to say that it is never appropriate or never necessary to resort to the use of lethal force for the protection of the vulnerable. This refusal in principle to preclude the use of force is based not on a naïve belief that force can be relied on to solve otherwise intractable problems, but rather on the certain knowledge that the primary consideration must be the welfare of people, especially those in situations of extreme vulnerability who are utterly abandoned to the whims and prerogatives of their tormentors.[3]

The type of force that might be called upon on in such situations could be considered a form of policing rather than military action. This is not a vision for changing regimes or bringing in a new order by lethal force but a way to protect endangered peoples. Long-term economic, political, and social solutions will need to be found by peaceful means, not by lethal force. What churches seem willing to do, according to the consultation above, is to support temporary police action for humanitarian purposes only.

Even coming from a pacifist orientation, I find myself broadly in agreement with these proposals. I would, however, be more insistent that churches consider a variety of approaches alongside "just policing," such as nonviolent intervention, restorative justice, just peacekeeping, and just peacemaking. In these efforts, Christians ought to seek alliances with those, from whatever religious and humanistic backgrounds, who are dedicated to peace in our world. And yet, how we as Christians justify theologically our actions and commitments matters profoundly.

This is why, as I will propose at the end of the book, a spiritually transformed individual conscience, sensitive to communal discernment, is integral to ethical decision-making. God works not only through the community but through the individual conscience. We can see an evolution toward this position in traditional, then contemporary, pacifist thinking. Before considering how just policing might emerge from a pacifist position, let us look once more at traditional Mennonite pacifism and its attitude toward law enforcement.

Traditional Pacifist Teaching

What impresses me about traditional pacifist (Mennonite) teaching on nonresistance is how thoroughly biblically and theologically based it is. This is evident when one looks at a work such as Guy F. Hershberger's *War, Peace, and Nonresistance*.

The fundamental moral law of the Old Covenant, according to Hershberger, is reflected in the Ten Commandments (especially the imperative "Thou shalt not kill"), summed up as loving God and neighbor. This fundamental law, which for Hershberger means non-resistance, remains the same in the Old and New Covenants. The judgment and wrath of God are but the cause and effect of Israel's sins, and continue to be so considered in the New Covenant.

What we are left with are two standards, one for Christians and one for non-Christians. God through his "permissive will" commands sinners to be punished by sinners on a civic level outside the church. (Hershberger calls this the "sub-Christian" level). Moral issues, such as divorce, government, vengeance, capital punishment, the legal oath, and warfare are permitted and even authorized only as a concession to the sinfulness of God's people.

This biblical and theological reasoning leads Hershberger to certain inevitable conclusions concerning Christians and the state, including policing. The state, like the Old Covenant, operates in the context of a sinful world; its role is to administer justice and maintain order with the use of force on the non-Christian level:

The function of the state is clearly stated in the New Testament. It is to maintain order in the evil society. Paul says: "Rulers are not a terror to good works, but to the evil." In this capacity the ruler is the agent of God for good. Peter also says governors are sent of God "for the punishment of evildoers, and for the praise of them that do well." In what sense, then, are rulers ministers of God? Only in the sense that in the operation of God's law of cause and effect in sinful human society, which requires that man suffer the consequences of his own evil, society has found it necessary to organize a state and appoint rulers with the power of coercion.[4]

However, those who operate on the Christian level do not participate in the state's use of force, including military service or police functions. Although they are submissive to authority, pray for those in authority, pay their taxes, and do all those things that are compatible with their life of nonresistance, they "are to manifest that same spirit of love and nonresistance which took Christ to the cross to die for the atonement of sins."[5] They may be involved in many non-coercive activities of the state, such as health care and education, and are law-abiding citizens, for law is given for "suppression of evil and for the promotion of the public welfare."[6]

But the Christian cannot participate in coercive functions of the state, such as the administration of justice, prisons, police, or the military. It would therefore be difficult for the nonresistant Christian "to hold, with any degree of consistency, a major executive, legislative, or judicial position in a modern state," although there have been exceptions, which "should caution one against declaring it impossible to occupy an important state position and remain non-resistant."[7]

Concerning those who make a clear distinction between policing and the military, supporting the former but not the latter, Hershberger has this to say:

> While it is true that the motives of an international police force sent out by a league of nations to punish an outlaw nation would be different from the motives of an army under the direction of an irresponsible conqueror, the resulting violence and bloodshed in the one case would perhaps be little different from the other. At best, both the domestic and the international police are instruments for the maintenance of order by means of physical force. This is necessary in a sinful society, but is forbidden to nonresistant Christians who seek to follow the Christ who taught men when smitten on the one cheek to turn the other also. There may be intelligent and

unintelligent, or just and unjust, uses of force by both the domestic and international police. This makes the difference between good and bad government. But from the point of view of the statesman, as well as that of the nonresistant Christian, the domestic police and the international police, or army, are fundamentally the same.[8]

Hershberger, representing the traditional position of Anabaptist-Mennonite nonresistance, consistently defends theologically both (1) a strong state that needs to use coercion in the sinful world, within the providence of God but outside the perfection of Christ, and (2) an uncompromising, nonresistant church whose sole allegiance is to the life, work, and teachings of Jesus Christ, being inside the perfection of Christ.

I have some serious problems with Hershberger's position, especially his rather crude supersessionism, which sees the New Testament as superseding the Old; his un-nuanced distinction between the sub-Christian and the Christian levels (the fixed two kingdoms); the sectarian perfectionism with which he views the church; and his refusal to distinguish between policing and warmaking. However, I do admire his unabashed support of pacifism at all costs and his consistent theological defense of his position.

Just Policing

In more recent thinking about war and policing, Mennonites have felt increasingly uncomfortable with the Hershberger type of strict dualism between those who are faithful to Jesus' call for nonresistance and those who are involved in the divinely ordained task of the state to foster order and restrain evil.

John Howard Yoder, also a pacifist, moves beyond such a rigid dualism to argue for nonviolent political engagement. He represents the beginning of the Mennonite shift from nonresistance to nonviolent resistance and involvement in the struggle for social justice (see *The Politics of Jesus*). He is clear that the state has a legitimate calling to preserve the good and restrain the evil (policing), and that *potentially* Christians might be called to serve as police, although he has never encountered such a person.[9]

For Yoder, it is clear that Christians are called to the task of reconciliation; it is not clear that the task includes policing and being an agent of divine judgment. In my conversations with Ontario police who are linked to the Anabaptist-Mennonite tradition, I have been impressed at how they see their task as one of conflict resolution and peacemaking, not primarily as agents of punishment supported by the threat of a gun.

Gerald W. Schlabach, who comes from a pacifist tradition and is now a member of the Roman Catholic Church, has done some careful thinking about just policing and just peacemaking. Good policing, he believes, is an area where pacifists and just war proponents can seek convergence: "Implicitly, the goal of peace church activists and stringent just war policy makers alike becomes just policing—just policing, not war."[10] While he does not call for those in the pacifist tradition to give up their stringent adherence to nonviolence, he does challenge pacifists to seek ways of positively participating in government, pursuing just policing and just peacemaking in a way that is convincing to those in the just war tradition.

Although quite aware of the fuzzy boundary between certain types of war and policing, Schlabach makes a convincing case for the distinctiveness of each as "ideal types":

> *Policing* seeks to secure the common good of the very society within which it operates; because it is embedded, indebted, and accountable within that community, according to the rule of law, it has an inherent tendency to minimize recourse to violence. *Warfare* may also seek to secure the common good of society, of course. But because it extends beyond that

society through threats to other communities, it has an inherent tendency to break out of the rule of law. It thus cuts whatever slender bonds of accountability that would truly limit its use to "last resort." And this difference is only the beginning. For having cut loose, war usually jeopardizes not only the common good of international community, but even that of the society in whose name it is being waged.[11]

Schlabach imagines a society that could dispense with war but not with just policing. This policing operates on principles approaching traditional just war criteria, applying them both to domestic and international situations. This kind of policing is therefore effective not only for local criminals but for criminal terrorists in a "post-9/11" world. A last resort to some form of violence would have to be a possibility.

Here Schlabach differs from pacifists such as American Evangelical Ronald Sider who argue for a kind of policing that would never resort to lethal force. In a 1984 public debate, Sider argued his position against Anglican moral theologian Oliver O'Donovan, who is a staunch defender of the relevance of the just war position, even in the context of the Cold War. O'Donovan argued that war is sometimes necessary in the defense of a third party, and he considered Sider's policing without guns to be naïve.[12]

Personally, I agree with Sider's call for just policing rather than war and believe that policing can be seen as a form of peacemaking and peace-keeping. Yet I also recognize with O'Donovan that policing without the threat of force, even lethal force, is unrealistic. My position would be that Christians should support policing as an alternative to war, even though the threat of lethal force may occasionally be necessary.

Conclusion:
Some Theological Considerations

Christians cannot deal with the profound moral issues around war and peace, including policing, apart from the larger theological considerations that ground the Christian faith: the trinitarian nature of God; creation, sin, and redemption; human nature and responsibility; the church and the Christian view of history. To conclude this discussion on Christians and war, I want to highlight several theological assertions that have a direct bearing on how we might think *theologically* about the themes we have considered in this volume.

Three Manifestations of the One God

1. In God's first manifestation, God is revealed as *inexhaustible transcendent Mystery* (as creator and preserver of creation). In this manifestation, God transcends our understanding of good and evil, and thus also our own ethical systems,

including our views on peace and violence. God is free and has the right to give and take life, to reward good and punish evil. How human agency figures in God's taking of life and punishing of evil remains an enigma. The creation and preservation of the world is a free act of divine grace and mercy, contingent on God's will and not logically necessary. God, therefore, is not a pacifist in the strict sense. The Old Testament, especially, witnesses to this transcendent dimension of God, which we ought not to domesticate too easily through selection of texts and one-sided readings.

2. In God's second manifestation, God is *revealed historically* (as Logos, Word, the Christ). In this manifestation, God is the formative principle of creation, the redeemer and reconciler of all things. Jesus of Nazareth, in his incarnation as the Christ, highlights the loving and reconciling nature of God, showing us the way of divine mercy, forgiveness, and reconciliation, including nonresistant and nonviolent love. These reveal to us the inner heart and purpose of God for the world. As Christians, we are called to follow this Jesus Christ in private and public life. However, for this discipleship to be a possibility we need an inner spiritual transformation, the empowerment of the Holy Spirit. One could say that wherever true peacemaking and reconciliation occur, there the Spirit of God is present.

3. In God's third manifestation, God is *immanent, personal, transformative Power*. The Spirit of God empowers us to realize moments of nonviolent love, even in this fallen world of sin and violence. But the ambiguities of life continue, warning against fixed ideologies. Reinhold Niebuhr had it right when he said that none of our choices are pure and unambiguous. The Holy Spirit empowers us to live boldly in a broken world, transcending moral ideologies and narrow visions of reality. The atoning work of Christ, through the Holy Spirit, forgives us our sins, even our violence, without excusing them.

Final Thoughts

We live in a fallen world characterized by broken relationships, injustice, oppression, and violence, and threatened constantly with chaos, anarchy, and nonbeing. In such a world God has created principalities and powers, including human structures and institutions, to preserve life and being, and to restrain evil. In fact, creation itself is made possible by God's drawing boundaries and creating order out of the watery chaos.

Although these structures and institutions are themselves fallen, coercion being a sign of this fallenness, they are used by God to maintain order in a sinful world. Policing is one such institution mandated to further and preserve order, so as to make life possible. Therefore, as the previous chapter has argued, it can be supported within limits by Christians. While the military may often act in a policing or peacekeeping capacity, its engagement in war remains problematic for Christians.

Since policing, despite its primary peacekeeping role, is premised on the threat of force, the question arises how Christians, whose basic allegiance is to Christ's way of nonviolent love, can support it or even participate in it. We might conceptualize this, and theologically defend it, with a modified two-kingdom or two-sphere model: our primary home (the Christian church) and our secondary home (the pluralistic world, the public square).

The boundary between these two spheres is not as fixed as Hershberger would have us believe, but is porous and fluid. We live in both kingdoms and move readily back and forth between them, making decisions of allegiance on the basis of conscience. Sometimes we say yes; sometimes no. It is not that one kingdom is sinful and the other pure. Both participate in fallenness and sinfulness and wait for the ultimate reconciliation of all things.

However, as Christians we can say that our primary allegiance is to Christ's way of nonviolent love. No taking of human life can be justified in the name of Christ, although it may sometimes be a tragic consequence of society's task of preserving the good and restraining the evil. Christians may be called to participate in institutions, such as policing, that provide human security and protection of vulnerable people. This participation must ultimately, however, be left up to the individual conscience in conversation with the church community. A clearer Christian consensus will hopefully emerge as churches with different convictions wrestle with each about the use of force. An even broader consensus may emerge as Christians engage with other religious traditions in seeking alternative ways to peace and reconciliation within a world of violence.

We end this study with a return to the vision of the Hebrew prophets. Through their grim litanies of sin, wrath, and punishment runs a constant theme, like a clear stream through a devastated human landscape: the Messiah is coming and will usher in the kingdom of God, the universal reign of justice and peace.

> The people who walked in darkness
>   have seen a great light;
> those who lived in a land of deep darkness—
>   on them light has shined. . . .
> For all the boots of the tramping warriors
>   and all the garments rolled in blood
>   shall be burned as fuel for the fire.
> For a child has been born for us,
>   a son given to us;
>   authority rests upon his shoulders;
>   and he is named
> Wonderful Counselor, Mighty God,
> Everlasting Father, Prince of Peace (Isaiah 9).

Select Bibliography

Aquinas, Thomas. *Summa Theologica*, Vol. 2. Trans. by Fathers of the English Dominican Province. New York: Benziger Brothers, 1947.

Armstrong, Karen. *Holy War: The Crusades and Their Impact on Today's World*. New York: Anchor, 2001.

Bainton, Roland H. *Christian Attitudes toward War and Peace: A Historical Survey and Critical Re-evaluation*. Nashville: Abingdon, 1960, 1991.

Brundage, J. A. *The Crusades: A Documentary Survey*. Milwaukee: Marquette University Press, 1976.

Cahill, Lisa Sowle. *Love Your Enemies: Discipleship, Pacifism, and Just War Theory*. Minneapolis: Fortress Press, 1994.

Calvin, John. "Of Civil Government," *Institutes of the Christian Religion*. Vol. 2. H. Beveridge, trans. Grand Rapids, Mich.: Eerdmans, 1964.

Carroll, James. *Constantine's Sword: The Church*

and the Jews. New York: Houghton Mifflin, 2001.

"Challenge of Peace, The: God's Promise and Our Response." A Pastoral Letter on War and Peace, National Conference of Catholic Bishops. Washington, D.C.: United States Catholic Conference, May 3, 1983.

Church and Nuclear Disarmament, The. Project Ploughshares Working Paper. Waterloo, Ont.: Project Ploughshares, July 1984.

Digeser, Elizabeth De Palma. *The Making of a Christian Empire: Lactantius and Rome.* Ithaca: Cornell University Press, 2000.

Elshtain, Jean Bethke. *Just War against Terror: The Burden of American Power in a Violent World.* New York: Basic, 2003.

Finger, Thomas N. *A Contemporary Anabaptist Theology: Biblical, Historical, Constructive.* Downers Grove, Ill.: InterVarsity, 2004.

Friesen, John J., ed. *Peter Riedemann's Hutterite Confession of Faith.* Scottdale, Pa.: Herald, 1999.

Gingerich, Melvin. *Service for Peace: A History of Mennonite Civilian Public Service.* Mennonite Central Committee, 1949.

Hanson, Paul D. "War and Peace in the Hebrew Bible," *Interpretation* 38 (1982): 341–62.

Harnack, Adolf von. *Militia Christi: The Christian Religion and the Military in the First Three Centuries.* Philadelphia: Fortress Press, 1981.

Hauerwas, Stanley. *Against the Nations: War and Survival in a Liberal Society.* Notre Dame, Ind.: University of Notre Dame Press, 1992.

Hershberger, Guy F. *War, Peace, and Nonresistance*. Scottdale, Pa.: Herald, 1953.

Hornus, Jean-Michel. *It Is Not Lawful for Me to Fight: Early Christian Attitudes toward War, Violence, and the State*. Scottdale, Pa.: Herald, 1980.

Hubmaier, Balthasar. "On the Sword," in *Balthasar Hubmaier: Theologian of Anabaptism*. H. W. Pipkin and John H. Yoder, eds. New York: Harper & Row, 1968.

Janz, Denis R. "Political/Social Ethics and War in the Theology of Martin Luther," in *Creed and Conscience: Essays in Honour of A. James Reimer*. Jeremy M. Bergen, Paul G. Doerksen, and Karl Koop, eds. Kitchener, Ont.: Pandora, 2007.

Janzen, Waldemar. "War in the Old Testament," in *Still in the Image: Essays in Biblical Theology and Anthropology*. Newton, Kan.: Faith and Life, 1982, 173–86.

Kant, Immanuel. *Perpetual Peace*. Lewis White Beck, ed. Liberal Arts Press, 1957.

Kraybill, Donald B. and Linda Gehman Peachey, eds. *Where Was God on September 11? Seeds of Faith and Hope*. Scottdale, Pa.: Herald, 2002.

Lind, Millard C. *Yahweh Is a Warrior: The Theology of Warfare in Ancient Israel*. Scottdale Pa.: Herald, 1980, 169–79.

Luther, Martin. "Whether Soldiers, Too, Can be Saved," in *Selected Writings of Martin Luther: 1523–1526*. Theodore G. Tappert, ed. Philadelphia: Fortress Press, 1974, 433–77.

Miller, Richard B. "Aquinas and the Presumption against Killing and War," *Journal of Religion*, 82/2 (April 2002): 173–204.

Mornay, Philip. "A Defense of Liberty against Tyrants," in *The Protestant Reformation*. Hans J. Hillerbrand, ed. New York: Harper & Row, 1968, 222–39.

Müntzer, Thomas. "Sermon to the Princes," *The Radical Reformation*. M. G. Baylor, ed. Cambridge: Cambridge University Press, 1999.

Niebuhr, H. Richard. *Christ and Culture*. New York: Harper, 1956.

Niebuhr, Reinhold. *Christianity and Power Politics*. New York: Scribner, 1940.

O'Donovan, Oliver. *The Just War Revisited*. Cambridge: Cambridge University Press, 2003.

O'Donovan, Oliver and Joan Lockwood O'Donovan, eds. *From Irenaeus to Grotius: A Sourcebook in Christian Political Thought*. Grand Rapids, Mich.: Eerdmans, 1999. Part I: "The Patristic Age."

Raiser, Konrad. "Statement on the War in Iraq," *Oikoumene*, World Council of Churches, General Secretariat, Geneva, 20 March 2003.

Regehr, T.D. *Mennonites in Canada 1939–1970*, vol. 3. Toronto: University of Toronto Press, 1996.

Reimer, A. James. "Christians, Policing, and the Civil Order" and "God Is Love but Not a Pacifist," in *Mennonites and Classical Theology: Dogmatic Foundations for Christian Ethics*. Kitchner, Ont.: Pandora Press, 2001. Scottdale, PA: Herald Press, 2001.

_____. "Constantine: From Religious Pluralism to Christian Hegemony," in *The Future of Religion: Toward a Reconciled Society*. Michael R. Ott, ed. Leiden: Brill, 2007, 71–90.

_____. "From Denominational Apologetics to Social History and Systematic Theology: Recent Developments in Early Anabaptists Studies," *Religious Studies Review* 29/3 (July 2003), 235–40.

_____. *The Emanuel Hirsch and Paul Tillich Debate: A Study in the Political Ramifications of Theology*. Lewiston: Edwin Mellen, 1989.

_____. "Gibt es 'legitimat Gewalt'?" *Mennonitisches Jahrbuch 2004*. Lahr: Arbeitsgemeinschaft Mennonitischer Gemeinden in Deutschland, 2004, 34–41.

_____. *Luther's Politics: An Examination of Primary Sources Relating to Luther's Doctrine of the Two Kingdoms*. Unpublished research project submitted to A. Rotstein, Department of Political Economy, University of Toronto, September 1975.

_____. "Trinitarian Foundations for Law and Public Order." Unpublished paper, 2005.

Ruyter, Knut Willem. "Pacifism and Military Service in the Early Church." *Cross Currents* 32 (Spring 1982): 54–70.

Schlabach, Gerald W., ed. *Just Policing, Not War: An Alternative Response to World Violence*. Collegeville: Liturgical, 2007.

Sider, Ronald and Oliver O'Donovan. *Peace and War: A Debate about Pacifism*. Cambridge: Grove, 1985.

Simons, Menno. *The Complete Writings of Menno Simons*. J. C. Wenger, ed. Scottdale: Mennonite, 1956.

Snyder, C. Arnold. *Anabaptist History and Theology: An Introduction*. Kitchener: Pandora, 1995.

Tertullian. "On Idolatry," in *Early Latin Theology*, Vol. 5, S. L. Greenslade, ed. Louisville: Westminster John Knox, 1956.

Tolstoy, Leo. "Patriotism or Peace" (1896), "Patriotism and Government" (1900), "Letter to Ernest Howard Crosby: On Non-Resistance" (1896). In *War–Patriotism–Peace*. S. Nearing, ed. New York: Garland, 1973.

Wood, J. "The Concept of Holy War in Ancient Israel," in *Perspectives on War in the Bible*. Macon, Ga.: Mercer University Press, 1998, 9–34.

Yoder, John Howard. *Christian Attitudes to War, Peace, and Revolution: A Companion to Bainton* (Lecture notes, 1983). Edited version published as *Christian Attitudes to War, Peace, and Revolution*, Theodore Koontz and Andy Alexis-Baker, eds. Elkhart, Ind.: Institute of Mennonite Studies, 2009.

_____. *The Christian Witness to the State*. Newton: Faith and Life, 1964.

_____. *Nevertheless: Varieties of Religious Pacifism*. Scottdale, Pa.: Herald, 1971, 1976, 1992.

_____. *The Politics of Jesus*. Grand Rapids, Mich.: Eerdmans, 1972.

_____. *Reinhold Niebuhr and Christian Pacifism*. Scottdale, Pa.: Concern pamphlet, 1961.

_____, trans. and ed., "The Schleitheim Brotherly Union (February 1527)," in *The Legacy of Michael Sattler*. Scottdale, Pa.: Herald, 1973, 27–54.

_____. *When War Is Unjust: Being Honest in Just-War Thinking*. Minneapolis: Augsburg Publishing House, 1984.

Statements related to Project Ploughshares and Canadian churches can be found at www.ploughshares.ca/libraries/Statements.

Notes

Introduction

1. I am indebted here to the program notes and text of Benjamin Britten's *War Requiem* provided by conductor Howard Dyck at a performance in Kitchener, Ontario, on October 16, 1999.

1. Definitions and Assumptions

* For further reading see Bainton, Introduction, chapters 1 and 2; Cahill, Preface and chapter 1; Niebuhr; and Yoder.

2. Hebrew Scriptures: God of War and God of Peace

* For further reading see Bainton, chapters 2 and 3; Hanson; Lind; Janzen; and Wood.

1. Oliver O'Donovan also alludes to this: "Thus the Deuteronomic law developed the sacral conception in the direction of an elementary 'just-war' code." *The Desire of the Nations: Rediscovering the*

Roots of Political Theology (Cambridge: Cambridge University Press, 1996), 54.

3. New Testament: Jesus and Loving the Enemy
* For further reading see Roland H. Bainton, chapter 4; Cahill, chapter 2; and Yoder.

4. Early Church: Divided Evidence
* For further reading see Roland H. Bainton, 85–93; Cahill, chapter 3; Harnack; Hornus; O'Donovan and O'Donovan Part 1; Ruyter; and Tertullian.

    1. Tertullian. *On Idolatry*, 102–3.

    2. Harnack, *Militia Christi*, 85.

    3. Ibid., 87.

5. Constantian Shift: The Justifiable War
* For further reading see Bainton, chapter 6; Cahill, chapter 4; Carroll; Digeser; O'Donovan; Reimer; and Yoder.

    1. Carroll, 175.

    2. Ibid.

    3. Oliver O'Donovan argues that just war theory was systematized in the early modern period (sixteenth and seventeenth centuries) according to seven criteria (five conditions for war and two for conduct). Just conditions: authority, just cause, intention, last resort, and prospect of success. Just conduct in war: discrimination and proportion. *The Just War Revisited*, 14.

6. Middle Ages: From Just War to Crusade

* For further reading see Aquinas; Armstrong; Bainton chapter 7; Brundage; Cahill, chapter 5; Miller; O'Donovan and O'Donavan Part 3; and Yoder.

1. Yoder, 25.
2. Miller, 203.
3. Brundage, 19.
4. Ibid., 20.
5. Ibid., 91–93.
6. Bainton, 112.
7. Armstrong, 152–53.
8. Bainton, 120.

7. Reformation: The Magisterial Reformers

* For further reading see Bainton, chapter 9; Cahill, chapter 6; Calvin, 650–675; Janz, 239–55; Luther, 433–77; Mornay, 222–39; Reimer, *Luther's Politics*; Reimer, *Emanuel Hirsch*.

1. For a study of two Lutheran theologians who made opposite political choices in the Hitler period, see A. James Reimer, *The Emanuel Hirsch and Paul Tillich Debate*, as cited below.
2. Calvin, 652.
3. Calvin, 661.

8. Radical Reformation: From Revolution to Pacifism

* For further reading see Finger, 289–301; Friesen; Hubmaier, 492–523; Müntzer, 11–32; Reimer, "Denominational Apologetics," 235–40; Simons; Snyder; Yoder, "Schleitheim Brotherly Union," 27–54.

1. Yoder, 38.
2. Friesen, 130.
3. Ibid., 133.
4. Simons, 45.
5. Ibid., 193.
6. Hubmaier, 499.
7. Ibid., 498.
8. Ibid., 501.
9. Ibid., 506.
10. Ibid., 515.

9. Enlightenment: Humanism and Peace

* For further reading see Bainton, chapter 11; Cahill chapters 7 and 8; Kant; Tolstoy; Yoder.

1. Cahill, 146.
2. Kant, 46.
3. Kant, 57–58.
4. Tolstoy, 68.
5. Tolstoy, 83.
6. Ibid., 115.
7. Ibid., 119.
8. Ibid., 124.

10. Twentieth Century I: Age of Realism

* For further reading see Bainton, chapter 12; Cahill, chapter 9; Gingerich; Niebuhr (1940), ix–xi, 1–32; Regehr; Yoder (1961).

1. Bainton, 208.
2. Ibid., 209.
3. Ibid., 215.
4. Ibid., 220.
5. Regehr, 35.

6. Cited in Bainton, 225.

7. Niebuhr, ix.

8. Ibid., x.

9. Ibid., 2.

10. Ibid., 14.

11. Twentieth Century II: Nuclear Pacifism

* For further reading see Cahill, chapter 10; Hauerwas, chapter 10; "Challenge of Peace"; "Church and Nuclear Disarmament."

1. Ploughshares, 1.

2. Ibid., 3.

3. Ibid., 12–13.

4. Ibid., 18.

5. Ibid., 15.

6. Ibid., 17.

7. Catholic Bishops, v.

8. Ibid., vii.

9. Ibid., iii.

10. Hauerwas, chapter 10.

11. Catholic Bishops, 7.

12. Ibid., 27.

13. Ibid., 37.

14. Ibid., 25.

12. Postmodernity: Terror and the War on Terror

* For further reading see Elshtain; Kraybill; Raiser; O'Donovan.

1. Kraybill and Peachey, 190.

2. "A Call by the Canadian Ecumenical Community against War with Iraq," The Ploughshares

Monitor, Autumn 2002 (www.ploughshares.ca/libraries/Statements).

3. "Presentation on Iraq to the House of Commons Standing Committee on Foreign Affairs and International Trade" (www.ploughshares.ca/libraries/Statements). "Prepare for Peace in Iraq," mentioned in the next paragraph, can also be found on the Ploughshares website, along with responses.

4. "Message from Church Leaders United against the War in Iraq," World Council of Churches (www.oikoumene.org). The Ploughshares press release, "Church Leaders United against War in Iraq," is at www.ploughshares.ca/libraries/Statements.

5. "NGOs applaud Prime Minister's decision," (www.ploughshares.ca/libraries/Statements).

6. Konrad Raiser, "Statement on the War in Iraq," *Oikoumene*, 20 March 2003.

7. Elshtain, 18–20.

8. Ibid., 23.

9. Ibid., 24.

10. Ibid., 55–56.

11. Ibid., 59.

12. "What We Are Fighting For," 182–83.

13. Ibid., 192.

13. Policing, Human Security, and the Responsibility to Protect

* For further reading see Hershberger; Reimer, "Christians, Policing, and the Civil Order" and "God Is Love but Not a Pacifist"; Reimer, "Gibt es 'legitimat Gewalt'?"; Reimer, "Trinitarian Foun-

dations," 1–5; Sider; Yoder, *Christian Witness, Nevertheless, Politics of Jesus.*

1. This chapter and the Conclusion are adapted from my essay, "Pacifism, Policing, and Individual Conscience," in *The Conrad Grebel Review: Mennonites and Policing: An Ongoing Conversation* 26/2 (Spring 2008), 129–41.

2. Michael J. Iafrate, a student of mine at the Toronto School of Theology in 2007, argues in a compelling essay that the American military culture promotes a community of discipleship that mimics many virtues of the Christian community but is in fact antithetical to Christian values. "Destructive Obedience: U.S. Military Training and Culture as a Parody of Christian Discipleship," to be published in an upcoming issue of *The Conrad Grebel Review.*

3. Ernie Regehr, "The Churches and the Responsibility to Protect," *The Ploughshares Monitor* 26/2 (Summer 2005), 12.

4. Hershberger, 54.

5. Ibid., 59.

6. Ibid., 159.

7. Ibid., 161.

8. Ibid., 174.

9. Yoder, *The Christian Witness to the State,* 56–57.

10. Schlabach, 18.

11. Schlabach, 69–70. Schlabach goes on to list numerous ways in which warring is distinct from policing: untethering from the common good, rallying-around-the flag, over-kill, failure

to meet requirements of law, use of greater and greater firepower, frenzy and irrationality, defense of honor, militarization of society, 73–76.

12. Sider and O'Donovan. The debate between Sider and O'Donovan took place at the Oxford Centre for Mission Studies in August 1984. Just days before, on July 28, Sider had given his historic address to the World Mennonite Conference assembly in Strasbourg, France, leading to the formation of Christian Peacemaker Teams, an organization which places pacifist peacemakers in war zones.